Coconut Lagoon

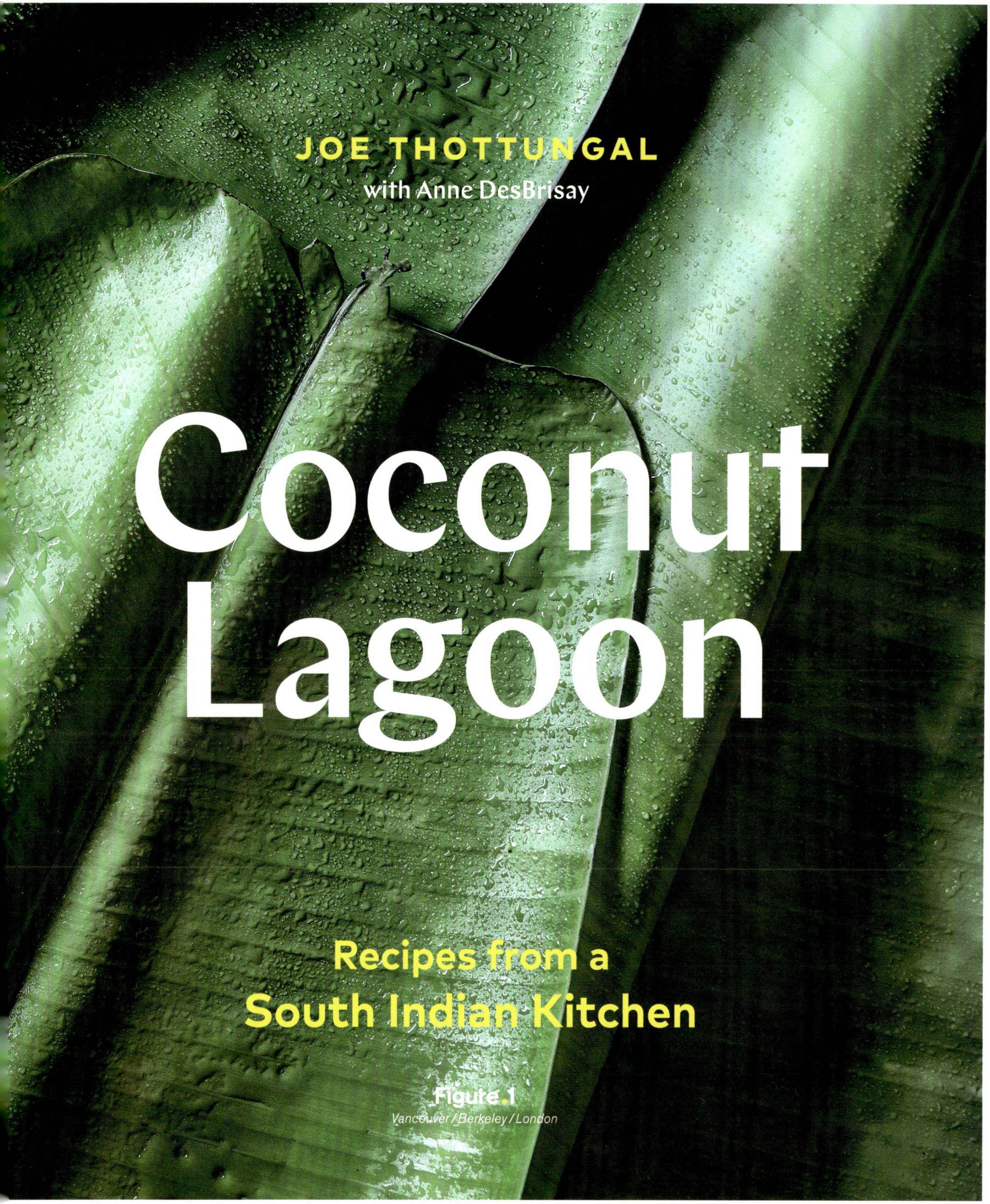

JOE THOTTUNGAL
with Anne DesBrisay

Coconut Lagoon

Recipes from a South Indian Kitchen

Figure.1
Vancouver / Berkeley / London

Copyright © 2019 by Coconut Lagoon
Recipes are chef tested.

19 20 21 22 23   5 4 3 2 1

All rights reserved. No part of this book may be reproduced, stored in a retrieval system, or transmitted, in any form or by any means, without the prior written consent of the publisher or a licence from the Canadian Copyright Licensing Agency (Access Copyright). For a copyright licence, visit www.accesscopyright.ca or call toll-free to 1-800-893-5777.

Cataloguing data is available from Library and Archives Canada
ISBN 978-1-77327-048-7 (pbk.)

Design by Naomi MacDougall
Photographs by Christian Lalonde, except for images by Jonathan Barker on the following pages: 6–7, 38, 40, 52–53, 62–63, 78–79, 116–17, 132–33, 154–55, 164–65, 179
Food styling by Sylvie Benoit
Prop styling by Irene Garavelli

Editing by Michelle Meade
Copy editing by Pam Robertson
Proofreading by Breanne MacDonald
Indexing by Iva Cheung

Printed and bound in China by C&C Offset Printing Co., Ltd.
Distributed in the U.S. by Publishers Group West

Figure 1 Publishing Inc.
Vancouver BC Canada
www.figure1publishing.com

RECIPE NOTES
Salt is table salt.
All herbs are fresh unless stated otherwise.
Curry leaves are always fresh.
Produce is always medium-sized unless stated otherwise.
Milk is always 2 percent.

Contents

8 RECIPES BY DIETARY REQUIREMENTS
11 FOREWORD
12 INTRODUCTION
15 THE ROAD FROM KERALA
22 KERALA INGREDIENTS
38 EQUIPMENT
41 BASICS

52 **Breads**
62 **Appetizers**
78 **Earth**
116 **Sea**
132 **Land**
154 **Rice**
164 **Drinks & Desserts**

180 METRIC CONVERSION CHART
183 ACKNOWLEDGMENTS
184 RESOURCES
185 INDEX

Recipes by Dietary Requirements

DAIRY-FREE

- 54 Appam
- 105 Baby Eggplant Masala
- 178 Banana Fritters
- 156 Basmati Rice
- 146 Beef Curry
- 84 Black Chickpea Salad
- 89 Broccoli Thoran
- 87 Cabbage Thoran
- 93 Carrot and Coconut Foogath
- 102 Cauliflower Masala
- 55 Chapatis
- 134 Chicken Chettinad
- 109 Chickpea Curry
- 125 Coconut Lagoon Mussels
- 135 Cook's Curry
- 70 Crab Cakes
- 107 Dal Masala
- 143 Duck Kumarakom
- 108 Egg Mappas
- 118 Fish Roasted in Banana Leaf
- 144 Kerala Beef Fry
- 83 Kerala-Style Slaw
- 152 Lamb Korma
- 149 Lamb with Fennel Seeds
- 167 Lime–Poppy Seed Fizz
- 131 Lobster Masala
- 151 Malabar Pepper Lamb
- 110 Mango Curry
- 157 Matta Rice
- 90 Mezhukkupuratti
- 100 Mushroom Aviyal
- 136 Nadan Kozhi Curry
- 98 Nadan Vegetable Korma
- 113 Ooty Mushroom Curry
- 69 Parippu Vadas
- 59 Pooris
- 66 Potato and Spinach Croquettes
- 94 Pumpkin Erissery
- 64 Rasam
- 74 Scallops with Tomato Chutney
- 126 Shrimp Malabar
- 130 Shrimp Mango Curry
- 75 Squid Peera
- 65 Sweet Potato and Ginger Soup
- 129 Tamarind Shrimp Masala
- 122 Thrissur-Style Salmon Curry
- 159 Tomato Rice
- 121 Travancore Fish Curry
- 86 Vegetable Kuchumber

GLUTEN-FREE

- 54 Appam
- 105 Baby Eggplant Masala
- 156 Basmati Rice
- 146 Beef Curry
- 84 Black Chickpea Salad
- 89 Broccoli Thoran
- 87 Cabbage Thoran
- 171 Cardamom Chai
- 93 Carrot and Coconut Foogath
- 102 Cauliflower Masala
- 134 Chicken Chettinad
- 109 Chickpea Curry
- 139 Coconut Lagoon Butter Chicken
- 125 Coconut Lagoon Mussels
- 135 Cook's Curry
- 161 Curd Rice
- 107 Dal Masala
- 56 Dosas
- 143 Duck Kumarakom
- 108 Egg Mappas
- 118 Fish Roasted in Banana Leaf
- 158 Jeera Rice
- 144 Kerala Beef Fry
- 76 Kerala Lamb Chops
- 83 Kerala-Style Slaw
- 97 Kerala-Style Vegetable Stew

162 Lamb Biryani	65 Sweet Potato and Ginger Soup	158 Jeera Rice
152 Lamb Korma		83 Kerala-Style Slaw
149 Lamb with Fennel Seeds	129 Tamarind Shrimp Masala	97 Kerala-Style Vegetable Stew
160 Lemon Rice	122 Thrissur-Style Salmon Curry	160 Lemon Rice
167 Lime–Poppy Seed Fizz		167 Lime–Poppy Seed Fizz
131 Lobster Masala	159 Tomato Rice	60 Malabar Parathas
151 Malabar Pepper Lamb	121 Travancore Fish Curry	110 Mango Curry
176 Mango and Sago Mousse	86 Vegetable Kuchumber	166 Mango Lassi
110 Mango Curry		114 Masoor Dal and Spinach Curry
166 Mango Lassi	**VEGETARIAN**	157 Matta Rice
114 Masoor Dal and Spinach Curry	54 Appam	90 Mezhukkupuratti
157 Matta Rice	105 Baby Eggplant Masala	100 Mushroom Aviyal
90 Mezhukkupuratti	178 Banana Fritters	98 Nadan Vegetable Korma
100 Mushroom Aviyal	156 Basmati Rice	113 Ooty Mushroom Curry
136 Nadan Kozhi Curry	84 Black Chickpea Salad	69 Parippu Vadas
98 Nadan Vegetable Korma	89 Broccoli Thoran	59 Pooris
140 Nilgiri Chicken	87 Cabbage Thoran	66 Potato and Spinach Croquettes
113 Ooty Mushroom Curry	171 Cardamom Chai	101 Potato Masala
69 Parippu Vadas	93 Carrot and Coconut Foogath	94 Pumpkin Erissery
101 Potato Masala	102 Cauliflower Masala	64 Rasam
94 Pumpkin Erissery	55 Chapatis	174 Rice Pudding
64 Rasam	109 Chickpea Curry	168 Sambaram
174 Rice Pudding	172 Coconut and Jaggery Crepes	175 Semiya Payasam
168 Sambaram	161 Curd Rice	65 Sweet Potato and Ginger Soup
74 Scallops with Tomato Chutney	107 Dal Masala	159 Tomato Rice
73 Shrimp Kakkan	56 Dosas	86 Vegetable Kuchumber
126 Shrimp Malabar	108 Egg Mappas	
130 Shrimp Mango Curry		
75 Squid Peera		

Foreword

I HAVE KNOWN Joe since his early days, and this book fills my heart with joy.

Joe is one of those rare Indian chefs who has experienced the world first-hand. He has been a chef at luxury hotels in India, Saudi Arabia, and Canada. He has also worked with prominent chefs like George McNeill, John Cordeaux, Luke Gagnon, Wilhelm Wetscher, John R. Stevens, and Giovanni Telles during his tenures at Hyatt, Canadian Pacific Hotels, Crowne Plaza, and Kempinski Hotels. And when he embarked on his own business venture with Coconut Lagoon fifteen years ago, he remained uncompromised in his ingredients and resources to preserve the authenticity of south Indian cuisine.

His homeland, Kerala, has been hailed as the land of spices, where vegetarian and non-vegetarian dishes are enhanced with fiery chiles, fragrant curry leaves, aromatic spices, and, of course, rich coconut. It's a region with Malabari, French, and Arabian influences, and staples such as pumpkin stew (*erissery*), dal curry, and dosas are delicious sources of sustenance and comfort. And at Coconut Lagoon, we can expect to see the same standout signature dishes prepared with deft hands.

With passion comes the courage to excel in anything: Joe followed his dreams, moved to Canada, and introduced an entirely new audience in Ottawa to his native Keralan cuisine. So it comes as no surprise that he has received numerous accolades for his food, including silver in the 2017 Canadian Culinary Championships and gold in Canada's Gold Medal Plates in 2016. He also contributes to his local community by taking part in various fundraisers and events, including The Great India Festival, held annually in Ottawa.

Indian cuisine comprises regional ingredients and traditions that date back thousands of years, so it gives me immense pride to be a part of this book, which introduces our heritage to a larger audience. We have so much to share, and readers can now experience the authentic flavors of Kerala with an unforgettable collection of tried-and-true family recipes—all because of Joe and Coconut Lagoon.

VIKAS KHANNA
Michelin-starred chef and host of *MasterChef India*

Introduction

MY FIRST EXPERIENCE of my adopted country happened in India. It was a 1998 conversation in Chennai with a Canadian immigration officer. "Cooks like you are needed in Canada," he told me during a long interview to assess my culinary skills. "You'll make it in Canada. You'll have a good life there." I was a twenty-five-year-old south Indian cook from Kerala, looking to take his knife kit... somewhere else. Where, I wasn't sure. I only knew my prospects for rewarding chef work in India were lousy. Maybe Australia, I was thinking: it was closer to home, it was warm... But here was this Canadian guy who seemed to really want me to come to his country, and his words were promising. Besides, my parents reminded me, there was that cousin who had an apartment in Toronto. He might put me up.

I knew nothing about what life might be like in Canada, but finding meaningful work seemed to be possible. I would be bringing with me my degree from a culinary college in Chennai and a pile of reference letters from hotel jobs in Mumbai and Saudi Arabia. The cousin agreed to share his basement flat, the immigration officer said yes to my application, and eight days after my visa arrived, I landed in Toronto to begin a new life.

That was twenty-one years ago. I'm now a Canadian chef, and the owner of Ottawa's Coconut Lagoon, a restaurant that serves the food of Kerala, my home state on the southwestern edge of India. Much of what is served in Indian restaurants in the West—ghee-brushed naan bread, marinated meats roasted in a tandoor, and the ubiquitous butter chicken—is typically north Indian, Punjabi-inspired. Like most countries in the world, India has many, many regional cuisines. Food from my region, however, wasn't on anyone's radar. At least not in Canada's capital, and I wanted to change that.

Fifteen years ago, Coconut Lagoon had a staff of three. Today, it employs sixteen, all long-serving, hard-working immigrants, including two of my brothers and my brother-in-law. It hasn't been easy. There were tough years at the start. People would walk in, see no butter chicken, no naan, exclaim "This isn't an Indian restaurant!," and walk out. But we were three southern guys from Kerala, determined to cook our own coconut-rich coastal cuisine. Eventually, that stubbornness paid off. There were a couple of positive reviews published, and people started coming. And coming back. And bringing friends.

I'm happy to say that Coconut Lagoon is now thriving. We've taken a junk-filled sports bar on a busy east-end boulevard and turned it into a place that people love, remember, and return to. We've been honored with good press. We have a wall of awards and recognition of which we are deeply proud. Our team has competed three times at the national culinary competition called Gold Medal Plates, taking a gold, a silver, and a bronze medal for our Kerala-infused dishes. Today, Coconut Lagoon supports my brothers who work with me, my team of cooks, bakers, dishwashers, and servers, all immigrants or refugees from Burma, Tibet, Kenya, Morocco, Sri Lanka, and the Punjab (home of butter chicken!), along with my family in Ottawa and back home in Kerala. And nowadays, instead of staring out the window, watching the cars whizz by, wondering if anyone will show up for lunch, we cook for a packed restaurant, seven days a week.

We have a good life here, and the daily pleasure of introducing my adopted country, and city, to the delicious food of my homeland.

With this cookbook, I bring that food to your home kitchen. In these pages are authentic recipes my grandmother would have served—including her Mango Pickle (page 50), Pineapple Pachadi (page 46), and a Thrissur-style fish (page 122). Our Parathas (page 60), Nilgiri Chicken (page 140), and Malabar Pepper Lamb (page 151) come from my long-time chef de cuisine, Rajesh. You'll find the traditional dishes served at the Onam sadya, our annual harvest feast (page 80), and ones we've created that pay tribute to the food of this region of Canada, both cultivated and wild, in recipes for a mushroom curry (page 113), mussels with coconut milk (page 125), and scallops with fresh tomato chutney (page 74).

Before embarking on these recipes, you'll need the right tools: the spices and seasonings that give our food its distinctive flavor. I've included a list of pantry basics, dry and fresh (page 22), a list of kitchen equipment you should have on hand (page 38), and notes on tempering techniques for spices on the relevant recipe pages. And because there is no Kerala cuisine without coconut, rice, and curry leaves, there are sections devoted to these essential ingredients (page 33).

The encouraging words from that immigration agent all those years ago I now agree with wholeheartedly: I feel I've made it in Canada. I am thankful to my adopted country, to the city of Ottawa, and, of course, to the wonderful diners who walk through our restaurant doors every day. This book is for them, and for all who are unfamiliar with the particular pleasures of Kerala cuisine. May you enjoy cooking these recipes as much as I've enjoyed preparing them these many years.

Nandi and *namaste*,
JOE

The Road from Kerala

I GREW UP in a large and loving working-class family in Thrissur, a mid-sized town a two-hour drive north of the port city of Kochi. Thrissur is considered the cultural capital of Kerala. Celebrations and festivals are a big part of life there. Family, friends, and food are fundamental to that life.

I left my home at nineteen, and though I visit as often as I can, life and work have taken me far from it. If I had to describe what I miss most, it would be the rains—the monsoons in June and October. During those endless days, there was time to sit and visit with family, to play cards, and to splash in puddles with my brothers and our friends. We fished in the swollen ponds, climbed our trees to pick cashews, and scampered through the damp laundry hanging in the house. The Southwest Monsoon in June known as Edavappathy coincided with the start of school, but at home, it meant fewer chores. My brothers and I wouldn't have to pump water from the well to irrigate our large garden. Our home was surrounded by trees—coconut, mango, jackfruit, breadfruit, plantain, pomegranate, cinnamon, guava, clove, allspice—and by curry leaf plants and pepper vines. It was a garden filled with life and fragrance, and I took it all for granted.

Walking to school each morning, there were other smells wafting from the open windows of homes and hotels: freshly fried vadas, potato masala with onion and green chiles, and our coffee, scented with roasted chicory. And then there were the smells of the markets. These I miss terribly. My mother would send her sons to the stalls every day: two rupees for vegetables for a sambar, another two for a bag of sardines at the fish market. We learned to smell the fruits, judge their colors and ripeness, feel the quality of the rice in our fingers, and haggle for a better price. Money was tight in our home, but there were always good things to eat, and always celebrations that centered on food and their seasons. Like most Indian women, my mother knew how to stretch a pound of beef, a piece of fish, a bag of shrimp. A little seafood would be mixed with plantain, the meat stewed with potato. One small chicken was a luxury, every bit of it used to feed many mouths, in a curry with lots of vegetables. And nothing was ever wasted in our home. Food was precious, food was preserved.

It was odd for a young man to choose a culinary profession. For my family, the only thing stranger than going into the hospitality business would have been entering the movie business. Though the kitchen was very much a woman's place in my culture, I knew my way around it as a boy. My mother worked as an office clerk at the agricultural university. This meant my brothers and I would come home from school with empty stomachs to an empty house. I started making snacks. Then getting things ready for supper—drawing water for rice, chopping vegetables, cutting up the fish—to lessen my mother's work, and to get food on the table faster when she got home.

I liked school, but I wasn't much of a student and that closed doors for me. I had a cousin studying hotel management in Bombay (now Mumbai). His program was expensive, but if I worked hard, he assured me, I could advance, have good work, and maybe travel to earn better pay. My English wasn't strong enough to go into service, but I figured if I learned to cook, I would always have a job, maybe see the world. These were difficult times in India. Unemployment was widespread, the country was poor, the workday long, the wages low, and there were no workers' benefits, plus very little opportunity for advancement. Although my parents didn't have a clue what a cooking career might mean, they helped me enroll in the college. I was the first in our family to leave Thrissur.

Three years later, having decided to specialize in continental cuisine, I landed a job at the German-owned Leela Kempinski Hotel in Bombay, where I lived with my aunt in her bachelor apartment. The work was difficult. We were more than 200 cooks in the kitchen, working ten to twelve hours, six days a week.

I earned the equivalent of about $100 a month. The training I received from Chef Muralidhar Rao, however, was brilliant. He was a young guy, super energetic and always on the move, never idle, never allowing us to be idle. I learned about banquet cooking and about staffing and overseeing big functions, and became more familiar with Italian and French cuisine. But there was little chance for advancement, and I needed to make more money. That meant leaving India.

Recruiters were looking for Indian cooks for jobs in the Middle East at the time, and I was hired by the Oasis Residential Resorts, which make up a walled compound in Al Khobar, Saudi Arabia. My pay jumped 500 percent overnight. My parents were thrilled. Plus, there were no taxes to pay, and nothing to spend our money on—no drinking, no clubs, no parties. Our amusement was watching TV and reading *Hello!* magazine. But I worked with great people. Every day was different and every day exciting. Our equipment and knives were all top of the line. Planes brought in delicacies I had never seen—fresh figs from Morocco, asparagus from Amsterdam, mushrooms from France, cheeses from Holland, fish from the Mediterranean. We'd fillet Dover sole at the table and serve it with almonds sizzling in butter. I learned how to make a proper Caesar salad tableside. I learned how particular the English were about their prime rib on Sundays, their cheese boards, and dessert trolleys. Still, there was no life for me in my walled compound in Saudi; no opportunity to marry or start a family. But going home for work wasn't an option either—there were no jobs like the one I had at Oasis. With my experience and qualifications, the options seemed narrow: Australia or maybe North America.

I chose Canada. Or it chose me. Seven weeks after my Chennai interview with that Canadian immigration officer, my visa arrived in the mail. Eight days later, on March 15, 1998, I landed in Toronto. And right out of the gate hit a devastating snag: I had $1,800 on me, and I needed $7,000 for entry. No amount of apologizing or explaining to Canadian customs that I had skills to offer, a cousin in Toronto, support from family back home, could get me around that shortfall. It was the requirement, the law, no exception. I was permitted to leave the airport but had one week to come up with the rest of the money or face deportation. And then an amazing thing happened: an elderly gentleman, a friend of my cousin's, heard of my plight and handed me a certified check for $5,200. It was all I needed, and I'm grateful for his kindness to this day. On March 18, I became a permanent resident of Canada.

The worst of Toronto's winter was over, but still, for an Indian guy, it felt cold and bleak. With my folder of résumés in hand, I walked to Yonge Street from my cousin's apartment at Broadview and Danforth and turned north. At every restaurant, from Bloor Street to Lawrence Avenue, every pub, diner, café, and hotel, I dropped off my CV. The next morning, chef David Lee called me. He introduced himself as the sous chef at Centro Bar and Grill. "Can you come and meet me tomorrow?" This time I took the subway. I showed him my letters of reference, and explained that I was new to Canada and ready to start work anytime. "How about today?" Lee asked. So I did. I worked fourteen hours a day for three days without pay. On the fourth day, I was called into executive chef Marc Thuet's office: he and Lee were happy with my work. They offered me $90 a day, flat rate, regardless of hours. It was a lot more than I was making in Saudi, and a ton more than I made in India, but one day's pay went to a Toronto transit pass, one week went for shared rent. So, I asked if they could make it an even $100. They said no, maybe later.

There wasn't much of a later for me at Centro. The days were long and grueling and I felt no sense of community there. I had no idea about the Toronto restaurant landscape and how Centro fit into it. (I discovered that it was widely considered the finest restaurant in the city at that time only after I left.) I only knew I was miserable there. So when I received a phone call from the Royal York Hotel—another place I had dropped off a résumé weeks before—to come in for an applied test, I jumped at the chance. They gave me a chicken and a bunch of asparagus and told me to cook something. I can't remember what I made, only that it got me a job. I gave notice at Centro and started as a breakfast cook, mostly doing room service orders, for the fancy 1,400-room hotel. The subway wasn't running at the hour I needed it, and buses came every thirty minutes, so I woke up at 3:30 AM to make my 5:30 AM start. But the hotel was happy with me: I was their trusted morning dependable, an immigrant who didn't party, didn't drink, was never sick, and showed up every day, on time, ready to go, knowing his stuff. When other cooks learned I'd started at Centro, they couldn't believe it. "You left the best restaurant in the city to cook eggs and make fruit salad?" I didn't care. I liked my work at the Royal York, and I was learning how to manage people properly by watching its executive chef. George McNeill was an Irish-American with a bright blue neckerchief and a style I deeply admired. He was kind, friendly, and super organized. His office was directly in front of my station, so I knew his routine well: he always arrived early and made the rounds, walking the kitchen greeting everyone, tasting and checking things and making suggestions. He worked to make the working environment better for his cooks. I was happy at the hotel and, besides, with my day ending at 2:00 PM, I could take on additional work. I started doing cooking demonstrations at Loblaws, did some weekend catering at the McLean House in north Toronto, and had an evening job for two years, cooking at the Park Hyatt on Avenue Road. I was making friends, sharpening my skills, improving my English, and sending extra earnings to my family back home.

And Toronto was beautiful. I remember that first year, watching summer arrive and the city blossom. Compared to my time in Saudi, where we never left the walled compound, this city felt huge and exciting. I would read the free newspapers in the subway, go through food magazines for inspiration, and sit in parks watching the world go by. But I was a single Indian guy in his late twenties. It felt like time to settle down and grow some roots.

I had been in Canada three years when I married Suma. She left her Kerala home for a small apartment in Windsor, Ontario, where I had work as restaurant chef at the newly constructed Casino Windsor. And then we made the move to Ottawa in 2002. I had landed a job at the Crowne Plaza Hotel (now Delta Hotels by Marriott) as restaurant chef, then was promoted to executive sous chef. In charge of the kitchen was Chef Wilhelm Wetscher, a fantastic boss, and a man who would become a mentor and a friend. He encouraged me to pursue my Certified Chef de Cuisine (ccc) with him, and, in 2003, we both received our ccc designation from the Canadian Federation of Chefs and Cooks.

My daughter, Marieann—the light of our lives, born on the day of the great Northeast blackout in August 2003—was eight months old when we opened Coconut Lagoon. My older brother, Majoe, had arrived in Ottawa, and with his training in hospitality, and some encouragement from chefs I admired, I felt the time was right to introduce Ottawa to the cuisine of Kerala. All my career I'd been cooking the food of other places—lobster thermidor, Caesar salad, Sunday roast with Yorkshire pudding. It was time to be an Indian chef again, cooking the food of my childhood, of my mother's kitchen, and reconnecting with that spice heritage so imbedded in my taste buds. There was no shortage of Indian restaurants in the city at the time, but they all served the more familiar food of the north. Ours would be the first to bring our southern, coastal cuisine to Canada's capital.

We started scouting locations for something we could afford. It took three months, but we found it in a rundown sports bar on busy St. Laurent Boulevard, a turnkey operation with tables, chairs, and a liquor licence. We pooled our money, got a line of credit and a $20,000 loan—as much as a bank would give me—and spent three times that much to build the business. We removed the pizza ovens, sold the mixer, bought new fridges, painted, and put up some Kerala posters. A week before we opened, I picked up Rajesh Gopi at the Ottawa airport. He was a well-liked cook in my in-laws' restaurant in Kerala, and I had sponsored him to come to Canada to help me. Rajesh, now a permanent resident with two kids in college, has been my right hand ever since, contributing enormously to the success of Coconut Lagoon.

But there were tough early weeks, when Rajesh, Majoe, and I would just watch cars speed by. We were averaging six people a day, mostly Kerala expats looking for the flavors of home. I could no longer afford Rajesh's rental apartment, so he moved in with Suma—who was now pregnant with Mathew—baby Marieann, and me. We three slept in one room, he had the other. And then came the first bit of press. It was from Gay Cook, a food writer at the *Ottawa Citizen*. She wrote about the cuisine of Kerala; about how different it was from the cooking of the north. A few months later, Anne DesBrisay, the *Citizen*'s restaurant critic, declared our food "worth crossing town for," and suddenly we were full. We were presenting dishes and flavors the city was unfamiliar with, and they were having an impact.

Kerala had landed in Ottawa.

KERALA CUISINE

So, what was it that landed? What is the cuisine of Kerala?

Its traditional dishes are born of our unique geography. Kerala is a slender slice of the Malabar coastline, blessed with abundant seafood, agriculture, and spices. Rice, fish, and coconut dominate our cuisine, in dishes enhanced with the spices for which Kerala is famous: peppercorns and mustard seeds, curry leaves and cinnamon, chiles, cardamom and cloves, kudampuli, turmeric, and asafetida. But our state's cuisine is also a product of a long history and rich religious diversity. Hindus, Muslims, and Christians have coexisted harmoniously in Kerala for centuries and each faith community contributes to the big, wide table. We celebrate the Hindu harvest feast of Onam sadya (page 80), cook the fragrant biryanis of the Malabari Muslims (page 162), and savor the Syrian-Christian delicacy of pollichathu, fish smothered in masala and steamed wrapped in banana leaf (page 118), eaten with our appam (page 54) and our matta rice (page 157). The routines and rituals of what and when we eat, in what combination and order, are complex in Kerala. They depend so very much on who you are and from where you hail, which landscape is now home, where your parents and grandparents and their grandparents are from, and certainly which faith you follow. Kerala is a tiny state blessed with many cuisines! It is my pleasure to introduce them to you in this book, to try to show them off and to give you the tools to cook what I cook every day. And then you should book your flight for a more generous education. My first home is a stunningly beautiful, historically fascinating, and utterly delicious sliver of the world.

THE SECRET OF KERALA COOKING

Cooking with our senses is second nature to Kerala cooks. And with practice, you will develop the confidence to judge the quality of raw basmati rice through touch and smell; to look for the ripple in the coconut oil that means it's hot enough to temper spices properly; to listen for the crackling sound of mustard seeds when they're dropped in that oil; and to know, by the aromas they release, when cardamom, cloves, cinnamon, and star anise are toasted in the pan.

What you should also know about our cuisine is that it is forgiving. These recipes are guides, they are not etched in stone. If you don't like a strong ginger flavor, add less. If you're a fan of a truly fiery curry, toss in more chiles. (And if you aren't, use fewer.) As for precise measurements, you needn't worry too much: every Kerala cook puts their own slant on a recipe, and I invite you to do likewise.

When planning a meal, you can certainly make just one dish and serve it with rice. (And making that dish the day before, to allow the flavors to settle and mingle and develop, is often a good idea.) But a typical Kerala meal will always involve at least three or four shared dishes, served family style. Typically, this includes a fish or meat dish, always a vegetarian dish, plus rice, bread, pickles, chutney, and yogurt. One dish will be dry, such as a thoran (page 87) or a foogath (page 93), and another one saucy, such as a dal and spinach curry (page 114) or Travancore fish curry (page 121). For those with special dietary requirements, I've included symbols to indicate whether a recipe is gluten-free **GF**, dairy-free **DF**, or vegetarian **VG**. Please note that this does not apply to serving suggestions or accompaniments.

It's very common in our cuisine that recipes develop to repurpose food: leftover cooked rice is stir-fried with spices and tomato (page 159), yesterday's roast lamb is turned into Lamb with Fennel Seeds (page 149), and an all-purpose curry sauce becomes a master recipe for surplus meat or a bumper crop of root vegetables (page 135).

You will learn basic techniques as you cook your way through this book—how to toast and grind spices, how to work with fresh coconut, how to temper spices in hot oil and how to cook perfect rice.

I cannot stress enough the importance of mise en place. That's a French cooking term that means "set in place" and it refers to having all ingredients measured out and ready to go before you start cooking. This is particularly key in Kerala cooking, as spices are added in rapid succession to hot oil. If you are rifling through the spice drawer for the fenugreek, the mustard seeds will be burnt. And there's nothing to do but toss them and begin again.

There may be errors in your initial trials. But keep at it. The rewards are many!

THE ESSENTIAL SPICE BOX

It would be impossible to imagine my life without spices. Cardamom, black pepper, curry leaves, cloves, ginger, coriander seeds, and the sour, shriveled, smoky kudampuli… These are more than the tools of my trade in the kitchen: they are the scents of my childhood, the memories of the brilliant peaks of color in the spice markets near my home in Thrissur, the comforting aroma of chai burbling on the stove for afternoon tea with friends. Nowhere is the spice garden more vibrant than in Kerala. It has been the hub of the spice trade in India for centuries, its ports their base, and the legacy continues with Kerala's spice production unrivaled in the world.

Kerala Ingredients

Some of the spices and fresh ingredients you'll encounter in these pages may well be unfamiliar to you. The Asian aisles of supermarkets are becoming increasingly longer and better stocked, as are fresh produce shops, but for essentials like Kerala matta rice, black mustard seeds, asafetida powder, and kudampuli, you will need to commit to some specialized shopping at an Indian or Asian grocery store if you want to truly cook this book. If you aren't lucky enough to live near one, or your town doesn't have one, consider ordering spices online. See page 184 for a list of reputable spice importers.

Always buy spices whole, as required, and in small quantities, and store them in airtight containers. In Kerala, we'd dry the spices in the hot sun. Here, we recommend toasting them in a dry pan before grinding them into a powder, to revive them after their long journey, or to temper spices like mustard seeds, coriander, fenugreek, and dried red chiles in hot coconut oil to release their perfume into the oil.

ADZUKI BEANS Also known as red cowpeas, these small red beans have a nutty, neutral flavor.

ASAFETIDA POWDER It literally means fetid, or putrid, so use this powerfully odorous extract from the rhizome of the ferula plant liberally at your peril: a little goes a very long way. In small amounts, though, it makes a lovely umami difference, particularly in fish dishes and dals.

ATTA Atta is refined wheat flour, a hard bread flour with a high gluten content, used in our poori recipe (page 59). It can easily be found in any Asian food shop and, increasingly, in large grocery stores with good Asian product aisles.

BANANA LEAVES The large leaf of the banana plant is used in ceremonial meals, like the Onam sadya (page 80), the harvest feast, and also to wrap foods, notably fish dishes, to be steam-baked. Available fresh and frozen.

BLACK GRAM (URAD) Black gram comes whole (*urad*) or split (*urad dal chic*), or split and hulled (*urad dal*). My favorite is urad dal, also known as white lentil, which has a creamy interior. It's a bean prized for its superior nutritive qualities and for its versatility in our cuisine—we use it in dosas (page 56), vadas (page 69), and pappadums as well as in soups, stews, and salads, where it lends a lovely little crunch.

BLACK MUSTARD SEEDS Not to be confused with either yellow or brown, black mustard seeds are considered a foundational spice in

Kerala cooking. Their flavor is released when they are tempered in hot coconut oil. If you can't source black mustard seeds, use brown mustard seeds, and use a little more as the brown seeds aren't as pungent.

BLACK PEPPER The king of spices! Kerala boasts the finest black pepper in the world. Highly prized since ancient times for its pungent, fiery taste, and once used as currency, the main "Black Gold" pepper production comes from the Western Ghats and Malabar region, though most Kerala homes, including my family's, grow the prolific pepper vines. It was one of my chores, as a child, to help harvest and sun-dry the fruit, to cut and re-pot new shoots, and, when the price was high, or we had a high bill to pay, to sell our peppercorns in the market.

CARDAMOM The so-called queen of spices, and my favorite, cardamom was the warm scent of my childhood. It is grown in our hilly country, near Munnar, and Kerala has one of the largest cardamom markets in the world. Our native variety is slim but packs a punch of aromatic flavor. It's pale green in color, with a thin, papery outer shell and small black seeds, and I use both the husks and the seeds to avoid any waste. Avoid black cardamom—these larger brownish pods have less flavor and are rarely used in Kerala.

CAROM SEEDS (*AJWAIN*) Closely related to cumin or caraway seeds, carom seeds are highly prized for their medicinal value. We use them in poori.

CASHEW NUTS Cashews love our climate, grow in abundance, and form one of our principal exports. Raw and unsalted, they're often used as a garnish or ground to a paste to thicken a sauce.

CHAAT MASALA Chaat masala is a spice powder mix frequently used in South Asian cuisine. Made with black salt, chili powder, cumin seeds, and dry mango powder, it has a distinct flavor that is all at once salty, spicy, and tangy. It's used for marinades and salad dressings.

CHANA DAL (*BENGAL GRAM*) Split brown chickpeas, these pale yellow, rounded legumes are used in our dosa batter. You may substitute with yellow split peas.

CHICKPEAS, WHITE AND BLACK They are known as "gram" in India, and we use both the white chickpea and the smaller—and, to my mind, much more delicious—black chickpea, or *kala chana*, which has a rough outer coating and is a terrific source of protein.

CHILES Fresh green chiles are ubiquitous in our dishes. Our Indian chiles are slightly bigger and slightly less powerful than the small and thin-skinned Thai or bird's eye chiles, though you could use either. The important thing is that they be firm and crisp. When we use red chiles, they are typically dried, and snapped into two or three pieces before being added to a dish.

Tempered in hot coconut oil, along with black mustard seeds and curry leaves, dried red chiles are essential components of many dishes in Kerala. Source chiles that are deep red and unbroken if you can.

CINNAMON Cinnamon is essential to our house Garam Masala (page 41), and used to bring a sweet perfume to curries, puddings, and sweets.

CLOVES A commonly used spice in Indian cooking, cloves are used whole as flavoring or blended into spice mixes. Sweet, pungent, and powerfully aromatic, cloves are also used in traditional medicine, soap, toothpaste, and perfume.

COCONUT (see page 33)

CORIANDER Aromatic with citrus tones, whole coriander seeds are dry-roasted to bring out their perfume. Ground coriander, in addition to flavoring dishes, is also a natural thickener.

CUMIN A common ingredient in Indian cuisine, nutty and distinctively perfumed, cumin seeds are used less in Kerala cuisine than in

LEFT TO RIGHT
White chickpeas
Adzuki beans
Black chickpeas
Black gram (*urad*)
Chana dal (*Bengal gram*)
Red lentils
Dal

the north. Toasting the seeds brings out their flavor. For a health boost, drink water infused with cumin seeds.

CURRY LEAVES (see page 36)

DAL (*DAHL*) Dal is the general term used for legumes. We use many dried legumes, whole and split, in our dishes—cooked with spices and coconut to make a "dal" or ground into a batter recipe for dumplings, dosas, and various fritters. Sometimes we fry dal in coconut oil to add crunch to a soft dish. See also chana dal, red lentils, or black gram.

FENNEL SEEDS The dried seeds of the fennel plant, they look like green cumin seeds and have a sweet anise aroma. Fennel seeds are used extensively in Kerala cooking, in Ayurvedic practices, and as an aid in digestion.

FENUGREEK Earthy and strongly perfumed, dried fenugreek leaves (*kasuri methi*) are used most commonly in butter chicken. A little of this ingredient goes a long way. Fenugreek seeds (*methi*) can be added to brines, curries, and soups. You'll often need to temper them to remove the bitter edge.

GARAM MASALA A masala is the name given a mixture of freshly ground seasonings. In our cuisine, we add garam masala to enhance flavor, and every cook has his or her unique recipe—its perfume like a cook's signature, the scent of his or her home cuisine. At Coconut Lagoon and at home, we use my wife Suma's recipe, passed down from her grandmother. Our Garam Masala (page 41) is a blend of cardamom, cloves, cinnamon, fennel seeds, and star anise. We make it every two days, using whole spices, first toasted to release their perfume, then ground in a spice mill. When we married, Suma took over the home kitchen. I would never suggest her garam masala needs more cloves... Never.

GARLIC You'll notice most recipes call for garlic and ginger, usually in equal portion. I recommend you buy good-quality garlic when in season; otherwise, look for a very firm head, with no soft spots, mold, or green shoots to indicate the garlic is past its prime. Store garlic in a cool, dry place.

GHEE To make ghee, butter is heated to separate the milk solids and water. Once the foam is skimmed off the top, you're left a hot yellow liquid that turns to creamy solid ghee at room temperature. Ghee is widely available in jars or cans, but is also a cinch to make (page 41).

GINGER When buying ginger, look for smaller, younger, thinner pieces with unwrinkled skins. The older the ginger, the more bitter the flavor. Also, ginger juice mixed with a little honey eases indigestion.

INDIAN BAY LEAVES (*TEJ PATTA*) Not to be confused with the Mediterranean bay laurel leaves you might have in your pantry, our bay leaves are longer and wider, with a sweeter, cinnamon-clove aroma. Source them at an Asian grocer.

JAGGERY Sticky, dark, and flavorful, this unrefined sweetener is made from the sap of palms or from sugarcane, which is boiled, reduced, and cooled into loaves or cakes. Jaggery looks like milk chocolate fudge and is used widely in our sweet dishes.

KASHMIRI CHILI POWDER Bright red and with a tempered heat, this is the powdered form of the dried Indian red chile, and is not nearly as fiery as the more common cayenne powder found in North America. In addition to adding a light heat to a curry, Kashmiri powder adds a beautiful color.

KUDAMPULI (MALABAR TAMARIND)
In Kerala, we use *kudampuli*, or Malabar tamarind, as an indispensable souring agent in our fish curries. The fruit, which looks like a mini pumpkin, is first seeded and sun-dried, then slowly smoked for weeks, until quite black and shriveled. You'll find it has a powerfully pungent smell before being rinsed and soaked in warm water. When cooked, kudampuli imparts a smoky, slightly sweet, and pleasing sourness (*puli* means sour in Malayalam) to a sauce. Kerala fish curry would not be Kerala fish curry without these essential properties. Note that in all recipes calling for kudampuli, both the fruit and its soaking water are used in the dishes. Stored in an airtight container, away from light, kudampuli will keep for years.

MACE The source of mace is the precious, scarlet-colored lacy covering of the nutmeg kernel, from an evergreen tree that produces both. Dried, we use it to add flavor and aroma to our gravies and biryanis.

MANGOES We use green, unripe mangoes in salads, chutneys, and vegetable curries. The ripe mango is used in our Mango Lassi (page 166) and Mango and Sago Mousse (page 176).

MUSTARD SEEDS see black mustard seeds

ONIONS The very foundation of Indian cuisine is the humble onion. You'll be doing a fair amount of peeling, chopping, and crying while making these recipes, but there is no getting around the need for onions—to flavor, to thicken, to sweeten, to provide the rich base of a curry. Unless otherwise noted, we use yellow cooking onions in our dishes.

POPPY SEEDS Soaked and ground, white poppy seeds are widely used in Malabar cuisine, often to thicken and flavor—particularly in vegetable dishes and milk-based desserts like Semiya Payasam (page 175).

1 Asafetida gum
2 Asafetida powder
3 Cumin seeds
4 Turmeric powder
5 Turmeric whole, dried
6 Indian bay leaf (*tej patta*)
7 Black mustard seeds
8 Garam masala
9 Red chili powder
10 Star anise
11 Garam masala
12 Coriander seeds
13 Chaat masala
14 Cloves
15 Fenugreek leaves, dried (*kasuri methi*)
16 Black pepper
17 Fenugreek seeds
18 Black cardamom
19 Mace
20 Fennel seeds
21 Kashmiri chili powder
22 Cinnamon
23 Kudampuli (Malabar tamarind)
24 Red tamarind
25 Green cardamom
26 Carom seeds (*ajwain*)

PUMPKINS Indian pumpkins are small and more yellow than orange. We use them in pickles, curries, and a famous Kerala dish called Pumpkin Erissery (page 94). When they're not in season or are hard to find, we suggest you use butternut squash.

RED CHILI POWDER Ground dried red chiles are added to just about all our dishes. It is not to be confused with Kashmiri chili powder, which imparts color more than heat. You may substitute cayenne powder, though it's hotter than our red chili powder, so use a little less.

RED LENTILS This quick-cooking pulse is a south Indian staple and used in many curries.

RICE (see page 36)

ROSEWATER Widely used in Persian, Middle Eastern, and Indian cooking, rosewater is simply water infused with the color, flavor, and fragrance of rose petals. Traditionally enjoyed in sweets and in milk- and dairy-based desserts and drinks, we find a few drops of rosewater also add a distinctive perfume to our Lamb Biryani (page 162).

SEMIYA (VERMICELLI) Our Malayalam word for vermicelli, or very slender wheat noodles, is *semiya*. Broken into short lengths, and toasted till golden brown, it's the foundation for the sweet and milky dessert called Semiya Payasam (page 175).

SESAME OIL We use toasted sesame oil for pickle making. Amber in color, this particular Indian sesame oil is often sold as gingelly oil or til oil in Asian shops and is not to be confused with the dark sesame oil made from well-roasted seeds, which has a low smoke point. Sesame and gingelly oil are made from the same seed, but the difference is in the process of extraction and the oils' usage.

STAR ANISE One of the star spices in our garam masala, star anise has sweet, musky, licorice notes and can be used sparingly in biryanis and meat curries.

TAMARIND Tamarind pulp is sold in compressed blocks. To create a paste, soften the tamarind in boiling (or very hot) water for fifteen to twenty minutes. Loosen it a bit with your fingers to help the softening process. Place a fine-mesh strainer over a bowl and, using a spatula or spoon, press the softened fruit through the strainer to separate the edible pulp from the fibers, seeds, and skin. Discard the contents of the strainer, and the paste in the bowl is ready to use.

TAPIOCA A potassium-rich, vital food for millions in the tropics, the edible bits are the tuberous root (which looks a bit like a yam) and the leaves. We make a delicious pudding with tapioca pearls, bathed in sweetened milk and mixed with mango pulp, called Mango and Sago Mousse (page 176).

TINDORA Also known as ivy gourd or scarlet gourd, tindora is a tropical vine that grows liberally in Kerala, producing a vegetable that looks a bit like a mini cucumber. You can substitute zucchini if you can't source tindora.

TOMATOES Tomatoes provide the juice, the liquid, the color, and the acid in a dish. If tomatoes are in season where you live, buy ripe, juicy ones. If the season is many months away, you may be better to use a can of good-quality whole tomatoes.

TURMERIC Used universally in our cuisine, turmeric has myriad health benefits and lends a golden color and an earthy, pungent flavor to many of our curries. You can also make the antioxidant, anti-inflammatory power of turmeric part of everyday cooking! Add it to water when cooking vegetables or rice, warm it in milk to soothe a sore throat, or add it to smoothies and soups. Buy it fresh, like ginger root, or in dried form and grind it yourself.

YARD-LONG BEANS Grown on climbing vines throughout Kerala, yard-long beans are the immature pods of the vines, and taste much like our green beans, but have a texture and lankiness all their own. If you can source them easily, you'll enjoy their flavor and crunch, but any recipe calling for yard-longs can be made with any fresh seasonal bean if they aren't available.

YOGURT (*CURD*) Called *curd* in Kerala, yogurt is eaten—with rice, with pickles—at every meal. And when I was young, every Kerala home would culture yogurt overnight using leftover milk—we never bought yogurt. In my Ottawa home, we culture our own yogurt, but at the restaurant we buy a good-quality, natural yogurt, and usually 2 percent. Yogurt is essential in my brother Majoe's famous Mango Lassi (page 166) and in our Kerala Raita (page 43).

COCONUT

Kera is what we call the coconut tree in our language of Malayalam, and *alam* means "land," so Kerala means, literally, "land of coconut trees." The coconut forms the very foundation of our landscape, our cultural life, and our cuisine. Its bearing on our state cannot be exaggerated! It grows wild along highways, arcs over our waterways, lines our airport runways, and dominates our beaches. Every Kerala home would have at least one coconut tree in its yard. In the kitchen, we consume its oil, its milk, its meat, and even its sap, but in Kerala, every bit of the plant and its hard-shelled fruit is used. The palm leaves are fashioned into brooms and baskets, the shells into cooking utensils and stunning handicrafts, and the dried bark is used as firewood.

COCONUT OIL In my Kerala home, we used no oil other than coconut. As a boy, my job would be to bring our own sun-dried coconut to the mill, then collect the pure virgin oil on my way home from school. At culinary college in Chennai, we made our own oil. Nearly all the recipes in this book call for coconut oil, so buy a good-quality, pure virgin oil, store it in a dry, dark place, and keep it away from water—otherwise, the delicate oil could turn rancid.

COCONUT MILK When added to curries, coconut milk softens bold flavors and adds a richness to gravies. Most commonly found in cans, here in Canada it's sold as coconut cream—the first extraction of the grated coconut flesh, without the addition of water—and coconut milk, which is the second extraction, with the flesh soaked in varying amounts of water. The latter tends to be thinner and have less rich a flavor. Coconut cream and milk—regular and light—are now widely available in mainstream shops, and there are dozens of brands. Some are purer than others, so read the label if you don't want a can-full of artificial thickeners, preservatives, and stabilizers.

At Coconut Lagoon, we buy coconut cream in powdered form. The powder stores better, there's no wastage, it's more versatile—we control the consistency and can use the pure powder in smoothies, sauces, and ice creams—and it's more economical. It's made from dried coconut meat, and we blend it with water to make a cream or milk as thin or as thick as the dish requires. If you're vegan, read the label carefully: some powders contain sodium caseinate, which is a dairy protein.

COCONUT, GRATED So many of our dishes call for grated coconut—aviyal (page 100), Kerala-style fish (page 121), the fermented batter for appam (page 54) and many sweet puddings. At the restaurant, we start with fresh, peeled coconut and grind it in a commercial grater imported from India. You could also grate your own using a fresh coconut and a box grater, or buy it pre-grated as a frozen product.

COCONUT VINEGAR Called "toddy" or palm wine in Kerala, coconut vinegar is created from fermenting the sap of coconut flowers. Increasingly found in supermarkets and health food stores here in Canada, we use it to add a sour note and distinctive Kerala bite to our vegetable slaw (page 83) and our Mango Curry (page 110).

HOW TO BUY A COCONUT

① When selecting a coconut, look for the three eyes and make sure they are dry and clean, without any moisture marks or black spots.

② Consider the weight. If the coconut feels light, it means the water may be dried out and the flesh inside rotten.

③ Hold it to your ear and give it a shake: you should hear the sound of splashing water.

HOW TO OPEN A COCONUT

① Using the blunt side of a butcher's knife, firmly tap the coconut around its equator (perpendicular to its seam), rotating it as you tap. After some good whacks, the shell will eventually crack.

② With a bowl beneath to catch the coconut water, insert the edge of the knife into the crack, then wiggle it a little to split the coconut in half. Drink or reserve the water.

③ To remove the meat, turn the halves over and give the shell another two to three taps to break it, until the meat will come loose from the shell.

④ Peel away the fine brown skin (it discolors the coconut milk and is hard to digest) and use only the white flesh.

RICE

The Kerala countryside is covered in green rice paddies. It is the most important food crop grown in our state, and is cultivated mostly in and around Tamil Nadu. We use five varieties of rice at Coconut Lagoon, all found at our local Indian grocery shop and available in most well-stocked Asian aisles of city supermarkets.

To clean rice, put the desired quantity in a large bowl and wash it well in cold water, using your hand to swish the rice around. Drain. Repeat washing at least two more times, or until the water is clear.

BASMATI is long, slender-grained, aromatic rice that's widely available in supermarkets. When selecting a brand of basmati, look for long, bright, clean-looking rice—and once you've found the brand you like, try to stick with it. That way you'll be familiar with the amount of water it likes and the cooking time it requires to produce perfect rice, every time. I tend to prefer the basmati rice from Pakistan.

KAIMA (which is sold by its north Indian name *jeerakasala*) is a small-grain, highly flavored basmati varietal, commonly used in the Malabar area for making biryani (page 162). You may substitute regular basmati.

MATTA also called Kerala red rice, is indigenous to our state and is our most iconic varietal, protected with its own geographical indication (GI). It is grown in the Palakkad district of Kerala, which borders Tamil Nadu.

PATNA is a mild-flavored, long-grain white rice. We use it for rice pudding (page 174) and for appam (page 54).

PONNI is a polished medium-grain white rice cultivated in Tamil Nadu that is used in dosa batter (page 56).

CURRY LEAVES

Next to the coconut (page 33), curry leaves are at the heart of our cuisine. They simply have no substitute, giving our dishes their unique citrus, herby flavor. They are generally used at the beginning of the cooking process; their essential oils are released in the coconut oil when fried. They are also dry-roasted and ground into spice blends or puréed in chutneys. Buy them fresh and bright green, still on the stem, from an Indian shop or some grocery stores. Stored in the fridge, curry leaves should keep well for about a week. You can also freeze them, still on the stem, sealed in plastic. If you can't source them fresh, at a store or online, buy dried curry leaves and double the amount required in these recipes.

Equipment

Here are pieces of kitchen equipment you'll find very useful in preparing these recipes. Some are essential, and others will simply make the job a whole lot easier! Start with a good, sharp chef's knife: there's a lot of chopping to do!

BOX GRATER One option for grating fresh coconut into shavings.

COCONUT SCRAPER The traditional coconut scraper is called a *chirava*. Its spike-edged steel blade makes quick work of any coconut shaving job. Alternatively, use the large holes of a box grater or pulse the coconut meat in a food processor.

FINE-MESH STRAINER For working with tamarind pulp. Once the pulp has softened in hot water, a strainer is used to separate the fibers, skin, and seeds from the usable paste.

FOOD PROCESSOR For making ginger-garlic paste in seconds, puréeing soups, or grinding coconut.

HAND BLENDER Perfect for making Mango Lassi (page 166) or mixing coconut milk powder with water.

MORTAR AND PESTLE For cracking or grinding spices like peppercorns, cardamom pods, or coriander seeds.

PIPING BAG Handy to have for piping out our Potato and Spinach Croquettes (page 66).

POTATO RICER For smooth and fluffy mashed potatoes.

PRESSURE COOKER A staple piece of equipment in any Indian home, its "whistle" is the call to supper! It cooks our food on average 70 percent faster than it would take in a regular stovetop pot with a lid, while conserving the precious aromas and nutrients of the food. Essentially, it's a whole new way of cooking and has its own language and method depending on the style of cooker. A heavy-bottomed pot or saucepan with a tight-fitting lid is the alternative.

ROLLING PIN AND BOARD If you're going to make chapatis on a regular basis you might want to invest in a small, round chapati board (*chakla*) and a thin, light pin (*belan*). Otherwise, a standard board and rolling pin will do.

SPICE GRINDER A handheld coffee grinder dedicated for spices is ideal. Store-bought, pre-ground spices simply don't have the flavor of whole spices, freshly ground, and these little devices make that task super easy.

SPLASH GUARD These round, perforated, plastic guards can be bought at the dollar store. I recommend them for tempering spices safely in hot oil.

TADKA, URULI, OR WOK *Tadka* is the Hindi word for tempering spices in oil or ghee. And a tadka is a rounded pot with high sides, designed for that very technique. They can be found online or in well-stocked Indian grocery shops. At Coconut Lagoon we use five or six large *urulis*, which are traditional cooking vessels of Kerala. These are more difficult to source, and more expensive. So the next best thing would be a flat-bottomed wok, with a handle. If you don't have a wok, use a small frying pan for tempering spices, then transfer to a larger pan to continue the recipe.

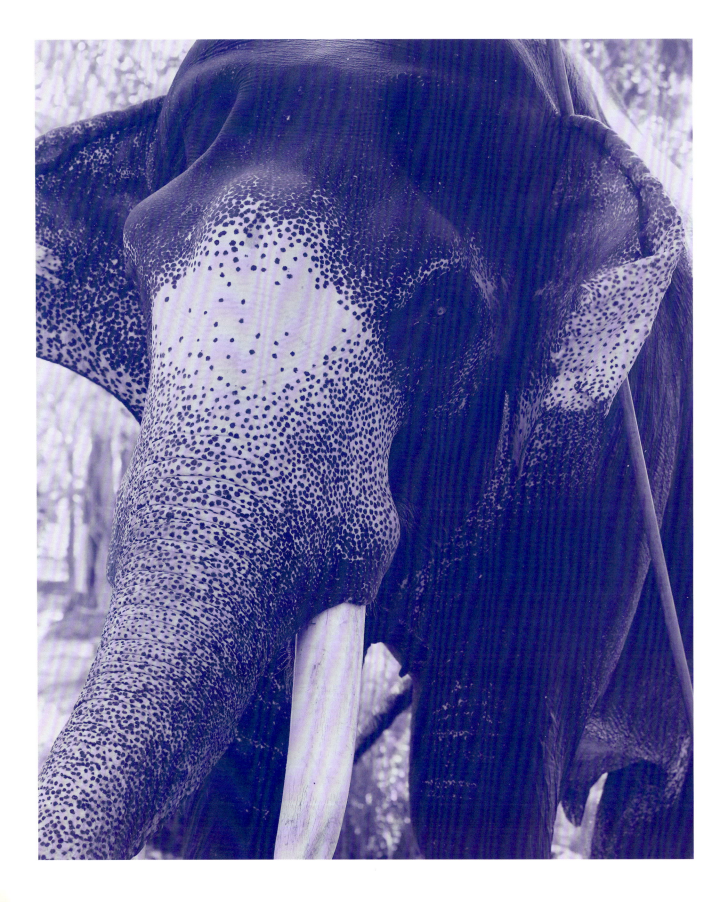

Basics

GHEE

In north Indian cooking, ghee is essential for cooking and for adding a delicious richness to a dish. Ghee has the lovely nutty flavor of roasted butter but can be heated to high temperatures without burning. In south Indian cooking, ghee also has pride of place, but is not used in everyday cooking. Rather, ghee is added as a delicacy to desserts, as a finishing touch to rice or a biryani, and certainly to show off prosperity and generosity on feast days. In my home, my mother, her sisters, and their friends would make ghee together whenever there was a surplus of milk.

MAKES ABOUT 1½ CUPS

2 cups (4 sticks) unsalted butter

MELT BUTTER IN a heavy-bottomed saucepan over medium-high heat. Reduce heat to medium-low and simmer gently. Every few minutes, using a small spoon or strainer, carefully skim off the milk solids that will rise to the surface as the butter simmers. It should take about 10 to 15 minutes for the ghee to turn a golden color. Pour ghee through a fine-mesh strainer or cheesecloth into an airtight container and set aside to cool. Store in the fridge for up to 2 months.

GARAM MASALA

Every cook has their own recipe for garam masala. This is Suma's household blend. Once you make it, you'll never go back to buying what goes for garam masala in the supermarket. Highly aromatic, it is used to bring extra flavor to many of our dishes, such as grilled steak or chicken, and it can be added to any stir-fry as a fragrant finish.

MAKES ½ CUP

1 Tbsp fennel seeds

1 Tbsp cloves

1 Tbsp green cardamom pods

2–3 cinnamon sticks, broken into smaller pieces

3–4 star anise

IN A FRYING pan over medium heat, dry-roast the spices for 2 minutes, until fragrant and toasted. Using a spice mill or a mortar and pestle, process the spices until finely ground. Garam masala can be stored in an airtight container in a dark and dry place for up to a week. (Any longer, you'll risk losing the perfume.)

GINGER-GARLIC PASTE

A fragrant and essential aromatic in most of our dishes, ginger-garlic paste is pretty simple to make, and a food processor makes easy work of it. While commercial blends are available in jars, they are watery and tend to include preservatives and stabilizers, far inferior to the paste you can make yourself.

MAKES ½ CUP

1 (4-inch) piece ginger, peeled and coarsely chopped (¼ cup)
10 cloves garlic

USING A DISH towel, pat ginger dry and transfer it to a mini food processor (or use a mortar and pestle).

Add garlic and 2 Tbsp water and process until smooth, wiping down the sides of the food processor as required. Stored in an airtight container in the fridge for up to 3 days.

FRIED ONIONS

Onions are the base—the very foundation—of Indian cooking, and yet here, they are used to add a crispy topping, as a finishing flourish to a dish.

MAKES ½ CUP

1 cup vegetable oil
2 cooking onions, finely sliced

HEAT OIL IN a wok or frying pan over medium heat until hot enough to fry. Add one piece of onion to test the oil (it should begin to sizzle right away). Sauté onions for 15–20 minutes, until golden brown. Using a slotted spoon, transfer onions to a baking sheet lined with paper towels. Spread onions out to drain and cool.

Store in an airtight container for up to 7 days.

CHILI-LIME SAUCE

The chili-lime sauce gives a lovely lift to our Crab Cakes (page 70) and Potato and Spinach Croquettes (page 66). Or use it as an accompanying sauce for fish and chips! A good-quality store-bought or homemade mayonnaise makes all the difference.

MAKES 1 CUP

6 cloves garlic, chopped

1 Tbsp chopped cilantro

1 Tbsp fresh lime juice

1 tsp red chili powder

1 cup mayonnaise

USING A HAND blender, combine garlic and cilantro and purée. Stir in the lime juice and chili powder, then fold in the mayonnaise. (Do not over-whip.) Chili-lime sauce can be stored in an airtight container in the fridge for 3–4 days.

KERALA RAITA

Our version of raita is thick, spicy, and flavored with chiles, curry leaves, and a hint of coconut. It is wonderful alongside a roast chicken, Malabar Pepper Lamb (page 151), or Shrimp Kakkan (page 73).

MAKES 1½ CUPS

1 tomato, sliced in half, seeded, and cut into long, thin strips

¼ red onion, thinly sliced (⅓ cup)

2 Indian or Thai green chiles, finely chopped

10 curry leaves, cut into thin strips (divided)

1 Tbsp fresh lemon juice

Salt, to taste

1 cup plain yogurt

1½ tsp coconut milk powder

Sprinkle of chaat masala or Garam Masala (page 41)

IN A BOWL, combine tomatoes, onions, chiles, the strips of curry leaves (reserving a few for garnish), lemon juice, and salt and mix gently. Put the mixture into a fine-mesh strainer over a clean bowl and set aside for 15 minutes to drain out excess liquid.

Transfer the contents into another bowl and stir in yogurt and coconut milk powder. Garnish with remaining strips of curry leaves and sprinkle with chaat masala (or garam masala) overtop.

COCONUT CHUTNEY

Making coconut chutney is a daily job at Coconut Lagoon. It's a must-have accompaniment for dosas (page 56), pooris (page 59), and appam (page 54) and a delicious condiment that cuts through the richness of fried dishes. It also makes a marvelous sandwich spread! Coconut is truly the star here. If using frozen grated coconut, thaw first, and squeeze out as much of the moisture as you can.

MAKES 1½ CUPS

1 cup fresh or frozen grated coconut

1 (½-inch) piece ginger, peeled and coarsely chopped

2 Indian or Thai green chiles

¼ onion, coarsely chopped

10 curry leaves (divided)

1 tsp salt

1 Tbsp coconut oil

2 tsp black mustard seeds

2 dried red chiles, snapped in half

1 tsp split and hulled black gram (*urad dal*)

IN A BOWL, combine coconut, ginger, green chiles, onion, 5 curry leaves, and salt. Transfer mixture to a food processor, add ½ cup warm water, and process until smooth. Transfer mixture to a bowl and set aside.

Have a splash guard and measured spices nearby. Heat oil in a small frying pan over medium-high heat until nearly smoking. Immediately reduce heat to medium. (You can test the heat of the oil by dropping in a couple of seeds. The oil is at the correct temperature when the seeds crackle, but do not burn.) Add mustard seeds and temper for a few seconds, until they stop popping. (Cover with the splash guard, if needed.) Add red chiles, black gram, and remaining 5 curry leaves and sauté for 20 seconds, until the black gram starts to brown.

Add spice mixture to the bowl and mix well. Store chutney in an airtight container in the fridge for up to 2 days.

MINT CHUTNEY

We serve this fresh summertime chutney with grilled meats, fried treats such as dosas (page 56), or a good samosa. You can make the mint-cilantro slurry well ahead, then add yogurt and salt just before serving.

MAKES 2½ CUPS

1 bunch mint, leaves only
1 bunch cilantro
7 cloves garlic
3 Indian or Thai green chiles
½ onion, coarsely chopped
2 cups plain yogurt
1 tsp salt

IN A BLENDER or food processor, combine mint, cilantro, garlic, chiles, and onions. Add ¼ cup water and purée until smooth.

In a bowl, combine yogurt, salt, and the herb paste and stir until smooth. Store in an airtight container in the fridge for up to 4 days.

Tempering is a traditional method of extracting optimal flavor from Indian spices, and it is a skill learned with practice! Reducing the heat a little before adding the spices prevents the spices from burning and adding a bitterness to your dish. If they do burn, simply start again with fresh spices.

Pickle making is a centuries-old tradition passed down through families from generation to generation. More than a way to preserve vegetables and fruits at their freshest and ripest, pickles are an essential condiment in our cuisine, and no Kerala home would be without *bharanis* (ceramic jars) of freshly made pickles maturing on sunny window ledges. Pick fruit at its ripest, and seasonal vegetables at their most vibrant. The salt, oil, and spices play vital roles in preserving, drawing moisture, and adding flavor. In the north, mustard oil is mainly used in pickle making, but Keralites prefer gingelly or sesame oil.

Always use a clean, sterilized jar for pickling and always wipe the rim of the jar clean before putting the lid on. They are best left to mature for at least 2 weeks before using. Once opened, store them in the fridge for up to 1 month.

PINEAPPLE PACHADI

Pineapples grow in abundance in Kerala. Sweet, sour, and fairly spicy, pineapple pachadi is an essential part of the traditional Onam sadya and makes for a sensible side with heavier dishes like Lamb Biryani (page 162) or Beef Curry (page 146).

SERVES 4

Tempered spices
1 Tbsp coconut oil

½ tsp black mustard seeds

5 curry leaves

2 dried red chiles, snapped in half

Pinch of red chili powder

Pinch of ground turmeric

Pineapple pachadi
2 cups fresh pineapple chunks

8 curry leaves

1 (½-inch) piece ginger, peeled and cut into thin matchsticks

1 tsp salt

½ tsp ground turmeric

½ cup fresh or frozen grated coconut

½ tsp cumin seeds

¼ cup plain yogurt

10 seedless red and green grapes, halved, plus extra red grapes for garnish (optional)

Tempered Spices (see here)

Tempered spices Have a splash guard and measured spices nearby. Heat oil in a small frying pan over medium-high heat until nearly smoking. Immediately reduce heat to medium. (You can test the heat of the oil by dropping in a couple of seeds. The oil is at the correct temperature when the seeds crackle, but do not burn.) Add mustard seeds and temper for a few seconds, until they stop popping. (Cover with the splash guard, if needed.) Add curry leaves and chiles and cook for 30 seconds more until the leaves curl. Stir in chili powder and turmeric. Set aside.

Pineapple pachadi In a small saucepan over medium heat, combine pineapple, curry leaves, ginger, salt, turmeric, and just enough water to cover. Bring the mixture to a boil, stirring gently. Reduce heat, cover, and simmer for 10 minutes, until pineapple is softened. Remove from heat.

In a food processor, combine coconut and cumin and purée to a smooth paste. Add paste to the pineapple mixture, then stir in yogurt and grapes. Heat mixture over medium heat and stir for 2 minutes. Transfer to a serving bowl.

Pour the tempered spices over the pachadi. Garnish with extra red grapes (if using).

CARROT PICKLE

Our carrot pickle is a zesty condiment that adds spark to any meal. Tangy, sour, and sweet, it can be served with grilled seafood, a good fish curry (page 121), Nadan Vegetable Korma (page 98), or Dal Masala (page 107). The carrots can also be substituted with an equal quantity of mushrooms or beets.

MAKES 2 CUPS

Tempered spices
3 Tbsp vegetable oil

1½ tsp black mustard seeds

1 tsp fenugreek seeds

4 cloves garlic, finely chopped

1 (1½-inch) piece ginger, peeled and finely chopped

12 curry leaves

4 Indian or Thai green chiles, halved lengthwise

Carrot pickle
2 carrots, cut into thin matchsticks

Tempered Spices (see here)

1 Tbsp Kashmiri chili powder

1 tsp ground turmeric

1 cup white vinegar

1½ tsp salt

½ tsp asafetida powder

Tempered spices Have a splash guard and measured spices nearby. Heat oil in a small frying pan over medium-high heat, until nearly smoking. Immediately reduce heat to medium. (You can test the heat of the oil by dropping in a couple of seeds. The oil is at the correct temperature when the seeds crackle, but do not burn.) Add mustard seeds and temper for a few seconds, until they stop popping. (Cover with the splash guard, if needed.) Add fenugreek seeds, garlic, ginger, curry leaves, and chiles and sauté for 1 minute, until curry leaves turn a brilliant green. Transfer to a heavy-bottomed saucepan.

Carrot pickle Add carrots to the pan of spices and sauté over medium heat for 1 minute, so carrots are well coated. Stir in chili powder and turmeric and cook for 1 more minute, or until the raw smell is cooked off.

Pour in vinegar and ¾ cup water and simmer for 2 minutes. Remove from heat. Stir in salt and asafetida. Set aside to cool.

Store pickle in a sterilized glass jar with a tight-fitting lid in the fridge for at least 2 weeks to develop the flavors. Once opened, use within a month.

1 Mango pickle
2 Garam masala
3 Chili-lime sauce
4 Lemon and date pickle
5 Mint chutney
6 Pineapple pachadi
7 Kerala raita
8 Carrot pickle
9 Coconut chutney

MANGO PICKLE

This is one of my favorite pickles—I love the sourness of the mangoes, the heat from the chili powder, and the wonderful perfume from the mustard seeds, fenugreek, and asafetida. This is my mother's recipe, passed down from her mother, and then to my wife, Suma, as a wedding gift.

MAKES 2–3 CUPS

Tempered spices
½ cup gingelly oil or sesame oil
1 Tbsp black mustard seeds
1 Tbsp fenugreek seeds

Mango pickle
½ cup garlic, finely chopped
1 (2-inch) piece ginger, peeled and finely chopped
3 Tbsp red chili powder
1 Tbsp ground turmeric
1 Tbsp asafetida powder
2 cups white vinegar
1 Tbsp salt
5 green, unripe mangoes, unpeeled and cut into thin matchsticks

Tempered spices Have a splash guard and measured spices nearby. Heat oil in a small frying pan over medium-high heat until nearly smoking. Immediately reduce heat to medium. (You can test the heat of the oil by dropping in a couple of seeds. The oil is at the correct temperature when the seeds crackle, but do not burn.) Add mustard seeds and temper for a few seconds, until they stop popping. (Cover with the splash guard, if needed.) Add fenugreek seeds and temper another 15 seconds, until browned. Transfer the spices to a heavy-bottomed saucepan.

Mango pickle Add garlic and ginger to a large saucepan and cook over medium heat for 1 minute. Add chili powder, turmeric, and asafetida and cook for 1 more minute, until fragrant. Add vinegar and salt, pour in 3½ cups water, and bring to a boil over high heat. Turn off heat, stir in mangoes, and set aside to cool.

Store pickle in a sterilized glass jar with a tight-fitting lid in the fridge for at least 2 weeks to develop the flavors. Once opened, use within a month.

LEMON AND DATE PICKLE

Despite the lemon trees in my mother's Thrissur yard, she finds the thicker rinds of "Canadian" lemons yield better results for her famous pickle recipe (and as a result, she always brings back as many lemons as she can fit into her suitcase). Lemon pickle is usually eaten with rice and fish curries, and here, she adds dates for a touch of sweetness.

MAKES 2–3 CUPS

½ cup gingelly oil or sesame oil (divided)

5 lemons, washed thoroughly and dried

2 Tbsp salt (divided)

3 Tbsp sugar

3 Tbsp red chili powder

15 dates, pitted

2 Tbsp white vinegar

½ tsp black mustard seeds, coarsely ground

¼ tsp fenugreek seeds, coarsely ground

2 Tbsp Ginger-Garlic Paste (page 42)

¼ tsp asafetida powder

HEAT ¼ CUP OF the oil in a heavy-bottomed pan over low heat. Add whole lemons and cook for 20 minutes, until skins are browned. (Turn constantly to prevent them from burning or bursting.) Add 1 Tbsp salt to the pan and gently toss to coat. Remove from heat and set aside to cool.

Wipe off salt and oil from lemons and cut each into 12 chunks, removing the seeds. Put lemon pieces into a clean bowl and add sugar, chili powder, and remaining 1 Tbsp salt. Mix gently to coat, cover, then refrigerate for 24 hours.

In a bowl, combine dates, vinegar, and 2 Tbsp water and soak for 6 hours. Put the mixture into a food processor and purée until smooth.

Have a splash guard and measured spices nearby. Heat the remaining ¼ cup oil in a small frying pan over medium-high heat until nearly smoking. Immediately reduce heat to medium. (You can test the heat of the oil by dropping in a couple of seeds. The oil is at the correct temperature when the seeds crackle, but do not burn.) Add mustard seeds and temper for a few seconds. (Cover with the splash guard, if needed.) Add fenugreek seeds and temper another 10 seconds. Add ginger-garlic paste and cook, stirring constantly, for 3 minutes, until the raw smell is cooked off. Transfer the spices to a saucepan.

Pour in 1 cup water, date purée, and lemons and simmer for 8–10 minutes. Stir in asafetida. Set aside to cool.

Store pickle in a sterilized glass jar with a tight-fitting lid in the fridge for at least 2 weeks. Once open, use within a month.

breads

ബ്രെഡ്സ്

54 Appam
55 Chapatis
56 Dosas
59 Pooris
60 Malabar Parathas

2½ cups patna rice, washed
1 cup cooked basmati rice
½ cup fresh or frozen grated coconut
¼ tsp instant yeast
1 tsp sugar
½ tsp baking soda
Pinch of salt

MAKES 15

Appam

അപ്പം

Uniquely bowl-shaped and made from a batter of fermented rice and grated coconut, an *appam* (or "hopper") is a Kerala delicacy commonly served at weekend breakfasts or on special occasions. The key to a crispy edge is to make sure you have a thin batter.

IN A LARGE bowl, combine patna rice and enough water to cover and soak for 4–5 hours. Drain, then rinse under cold running water.

In a food processor, combine patna and basmati rice, coconut, and yeast and process to a smooth batter. Add sugar, baking soda, and salt and mix well. Cover and set aside to ferment at room temperature overnight, or for at least 8 hours.

Heat a wok or a small nonstick frying pan over medium heat. Pour in about ¼ cup of batter, tilting the pan to evenly coat the bottom (if possible, the batter should come up the sides of the pan to achieve the traditional cupped shape). Cover and cook for 1 minute, until the sides are crispy and the white center is spongy but cooked through. Transfer to a plate and repeat with remaining batter.

Serve immediately.

MAKES 8

1 cup atta or finely milled wheat flour, plus extra for dusting

Pinch of salt

Chapatis

ചപ്പാത്തി

Nothing like chapati on a Sunday night with a beautiful Beef Curry (page 146)! The dough is a cinch to make, and the kneading is critical for a soft result. Cooked in a dry frying pan, this super healthy whole-wheat flatbread is a popular accompaniment to many of the dishes in this book. Traditionally, a *chakla* and *belan* (see Equipment, page 38) are used to roll them, but a large cutting board and rolling pin will do.

IN A LARGE bowl, combine flour and salt. Gradually, a bit at a time, add ¼ cup water, mixing and kneading, by hand, for at least 2 minutes, until the dough is soft but not sticky. If it becomes sticky, add a little more flour and blend it in. Cover the bowl with a dish towel and set aside for at least 10 minutes to rest.

Divide the dough into 8 equal pieces. On a lightly floured work surface, roll each piece of dough into a thin circle, about ⅛-inch thick.

Heat a flat griddle or nonstick frying pan over medium heat and add a disk of dough to the pan. Cook for 30 seconds, using the back of a spoon to press the surface in different spots, until bubbles form. Using an offset spatula, flip and cook for another 30 seconds, pressing the spoon from spot to spot. Flip again and cook until the chapati bubbles are pale brown. Transfer to a plate and repeat with remaining chapatis.

Serve immediately.

1 cup patna rice, washed

1 cup ponni rice, washed

½ cup split and hulled black gram (*urad dal*), rinsed

2 Tbsp chana dal or yellow split peas, rinsed

1 tsp fenugreek seeds

1 tsp salt

Ghee (page 41), for sprinkling

1½ qty Potato Masala (page 101)

To serve
Coconut Chutney (page 44)
Tomato Chutney (page 74)
Sambar (optional)

MAKES 10–12

Dosas

ദോസ

The closest we have to a French crepe, the dosa is made of fermented rice and lentils and is typically served for breakfast or as an evening snack. I think of my grandfather whenever I make dosas—they were a favorite of his, and my mother would always have the batter ready for his arrival. They are typically stuffed with Potato Masala (page 101), and are delicious served with Coconut Chutney (page 44), Malabar Pepper Lamb (page 151), or Cook's Curry (page 125).

IN A BOWL, combine rices, black gram, chana dal, and fenugreek seeds. Cover with cold water and soak for 2–4 hours to soften. Drain, then put mixture into a food processor. Add salt and process to a coarse paste. Pour into a large bowl, cover with plastic wrap, and set aside at room temperature to ferment overnight, or for at least 6 hours.

Heat a small nonstick frying pan over medium heat. Pour about ¼ cup batter into the pan. Using the back of a ladle, spread into a thin crepe. Cook for 1 minute, then sprinkle a few drops of ghee on top and flip. Cook for 1 more minute. Transfer to a plate and repeat with remaining batter.

Fill each dosa with ½ cup of potato masala and roll up. Serve immediately with chutneys and sambar (if using).

MAKES 20

2 cups atta or finely milled wheat flour

½ tsp salt

2 cups + 1 Tbsp vegetable oil (divided), plus extra for rubbing and greasing

1 tsp carom seeds (*ajwain*)

Pooris

പൂരി

This north Indian bread was always a weekend breakfast treat for my brothers and me. We'd roll out the dough for our mother, and she'd fry up the pooris, one by one, doing her best to keep up with demand. We could eat three or four each, then look up, hopeful of one more. I recommend serving them with Potato Masala (page 101) or Egg Mappas (page 108).

SIFT FLOUR INTO a large bowl. Add salt, 1 Tbsp oil, and carom seeds and mix well.

Have 1 cup of water on hand. Drizzle 1–2 Tbsp water into the bowl and, with your fingers, incorporate the water into the flour mixture. Repeat until all the water is used and the dough comes together. Knead the dough in the bowl for 5–7 minutes, until firm but still soft and dry. Rub a little oil over the dough, cover it with a damp cloth, and set aside to rest for at least 20 minutes.

Lightly knead the dough again, then transfer it to a lightly oiled work surface. Roll into a 2-inch-diameter log, then divide the dough into 20 equal portions. Using a rolling pin, roll a piece of dough into a thin circle, about 4 inches in diameter. Repeat with the remaining dough.

Heat the remaining 2 cups of oil in a wok or deep saucepan over medium-high heat, until the oil starts smoking. Using a slotted spoon, carefully lower a poori into the oil (taking care not to splash) and deep-fry for 10 seconds, until it begins to puff. Turn over and fry for another 10 seconds, or until golden. Carefully transfer it to a plate lined with paper towels. Repeat with remaining pooris, making sure the oil stays at temperature.

Serve immediately.

4½ cups all-purpose flour, plus extra for dusting

2 large eggs

½ cup milk

2 tsp salt

1 Tbsp sugar

¼ cup warm Ghee (page 41), plus extra for rubbing and brushing

MAKES 16

Malabar Parathas

മലബാർ പൊറോട്ട

Nothing says "home" to a Keralite more than a paratha. Coiled and layered like a croissant, flecked with char-spots, with a crunchy outer layer and a soft, flaky filling, it's our star bread, perfectly suited to scooping up coconut-rich curries or hearty meat stews.

PLACE FLOUR IN a large bowl and make a well in the center.

In a second bowl, whisk together eggs, milk, salt, and sugar. Pour the mixture into the flour well and combine using your hands. Pour in ghee and 1 cup room temperature water and mix until it turns to a slightly sticky dough.

Transfer dough to a lightly floured work surface and knead for 5 minutes by hand, until soft, smooth, and no longer sticky. (Add more flour if needed.) Divide dough into 16 balls. Oil your hands with a little ghee and rub over each ball. Cover with a clean towel and rest for 15–30 minutes.

Using a rolling pin, roll out a dough ball to a ⅛-inch thickness. Using a knife or pastry cutter, cut ½-inch-wide strips of dough. Wind one strip around your finger. Add a second strip over top and continue winding, until all the strips from one dough ball are used. Repeat until you have 16 raw parathas. Cover with plastic wrap or a damp towel and set aside at room temperature for 2–3 hours (this will create a softer dough). Using a rolling pin, gently roll out the raw parathas to the thickness of a pancake, about ¼-inch thick.

Heat a large frying pan over medium heat. Add a raw paratha and cook for 1 minute. Brush a little ghee on the surface, flip, and cook for 1 more minute, until the paratha forms light brown spots on the surface (from the caramelization of the sugar). Flip again a few more times, until both sides are golden brown and crispy. Transfer to a plate.

While the bread is still hot, and using a clapping motion with your hands, scrunch its edges toward the center. This releases the layers, making the paratha lighter and flakier. Wrap the parathas in foil to keep them warm, then repeat with the remaining dough.

Place parathas in a basket and serve immediately.

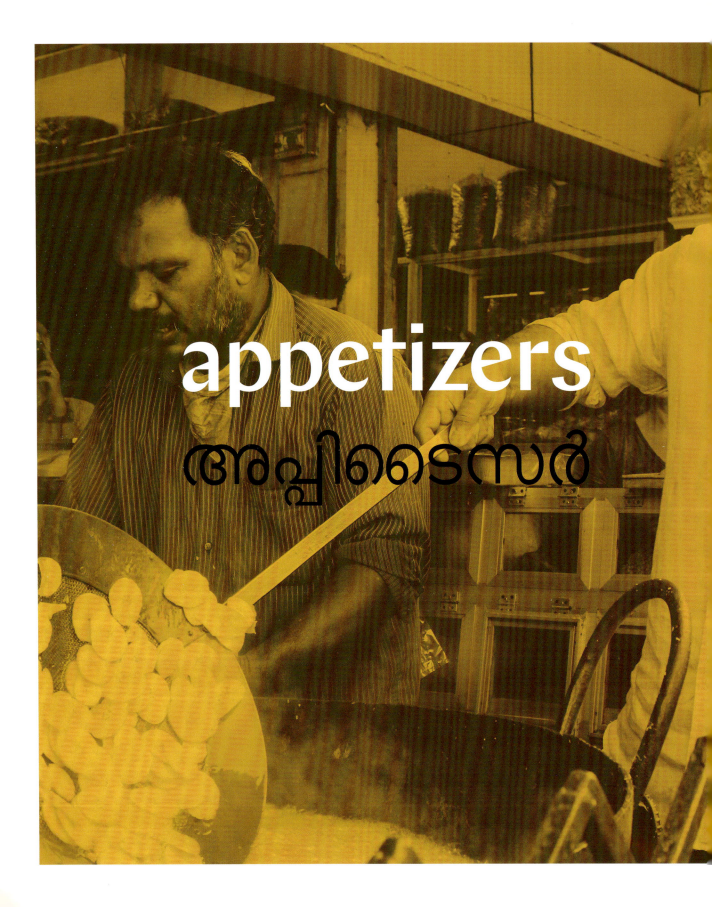

appetizers

അപ്പിടൈസർ

- 64 Rasam
- 65 Sweet Potato and Ginger Soup
- 66 Potato and Spinach Croquettes
- 69 Parippu Vadas
- 70 Crab Cakes
- 73 Shrimp Kakkan
- 74 Scallops with Tomato Chutney
- 75 Squid Peera
- 76 Kerala Lamb Chops

Tamarind paste
3 oz tamarind pulp, broken into small chunks

Rasam
1 tsp coconut oil
4 cloves garlic, crushed
2 dried red chiles, snapped in half
Sprig of curry leaves
1 tsp coriander seeds, crushed
¾ tsp coarsely ground black pepper (divided)
¼ tsp cumin seeds, crushed
2 large ripe tomatoes, coarsely chopped
Generous pinch of asafetida powder
Generous pinch of ground turmeric
Handful of cilantro leaves
1 tsp salt
Tamarind Paste (see here)

SERVES 4

Rasam

ഠസം

This traditional south Indian soup is peppery and sour and piqued with chiles—it will whet the appetite and cure what ails you. The word *rasam* means "essence" or "juice," but it also stands in for the word "taste" or "tasty." You might say a dish has good *rasam* and that would be a lovely compliment.

Tamarind paste Place tamarind in a small bowl, add enough boiling water to cover, and set aside for 20–30 minutes to soften. Transfer softened pulp to a fine-mesh strainer set over a clean bowl. Using a spoon or spatula, push the pulp through the strainer to separate the tamarind paste from its fibers (and occasional seeds). Scrape the paste from the underside of the strainer to collect as much as you can. Discard the fibers and set the paste aside.

Rasam Heat oil in a large saucepan over medium heat. Add garlic, chiles, curry leaves, coriander seeds, ¼ tsp of the pepper, and cumin seeds and sauté for 1 minute, until fragrant.

Add tomatoes, asafetida, and turmeric and cook for 2–3 minutes until tomatoes start to break up.

Pour in 4 cups water, stir in cilantro and salt, and bring to a boil. Cover and simmer for 3 minutes. Add tamarind paste, stir, and simmer for another 2 minutes. Sprinkle with the remaining ½ tsp pepper. Serve hot or warm.

SERVES 8

3 Tbsp coconut oil

½ cup chopped ginger

6 cloves garlic

2 sweet potatoes, cut into ½-inch cubes

2 carrots, cut into ½-inch cubes

1½ tsp salt, plus extra to taste

1½ tsp ground turmeric

½ cup coconut milk

Dried fenugreek leaves (*kasuri methi*), for garnish

Pinch of Garam Masala (page 41), for garnish

To serve
Pappadums

Sweet Potato and Ginger Soup

മധുരക്കിഴങ്ങ്, ഇഞ്ചി സൂപ്പ്

Mild, creamy, and comforting, this is our most popular soup at Coconut Lagoon. At home, we'd make it for monsoon season; here, it's perfect for our Canadian winters. Feel free to use butternut squash, more carrots, or even tomatoes instead of the sweet potatoes. I've always made enough for leftovers—the longer this soup sits, the more flavorful it becomes.

HEAT OIL IN a large saucepan over medium heat. Add ginger and garlic and sauté for 3 minutes, until lightly brown and fragrant. Add sweet potatoes and carrots, season with salt, and mix well for 2–3 minutes. Add turmeric and sauté for another 3 minutes, then add about 3 cups of cold water to cover. (If needed, add more water to cover vegetables.) Cover and cook for 25 minutes, until vegetables are tender.

In a bowl, combine coconut milk and 2 cups of water and mix well. Pour mixture into the pan, stir, and bring to a boil. Season with salt to taste.

Garnish with dried fenugreek leaves and garam masala and serve with pappadums.

MAKES 8

2 large potatoes, peeled and cut into 1-inch cubes

½ tsp ground turmeric

1½ tsp salt (divided)

1 Tbsp coconut oil

½ tsp cumin seeds

1 onion, chopped

1 tsp Ginger-Garlic Paste (page 42)

½ tsp ground coriander

¼ tsp red chili powder

2 cups chopped spinach

1 tsp dried fenugreek leaves (*kasuri methi*)

½ tsp Garam Masala (page 41)

2 eggs

1 cup panko breadcrumbs

2 cups vegetable oil, for deep-frying

To serve
Chili-Lime Sauce (page 43)

Potato and Spinach Croquettes

ഉരുളക്കിഴങ്ങ് ചീര കട്ലറ്റ്

We make croquettes with beef, lamb, or fish at home, but here, we've replaced the meat with greens. When the markets are filled with summer greens—spinach, Swiss chard, kale—we make these tasty little treats by the dozens and toss them in the freezer. At the restaurant, we find a piping bag the fastest way to shape them, but rolling them out by hand works well too. When ready to serve, simply cook the frozen croquettes in hot oil.

COMBINE POTATOES, TURMERIC, and 1 tsp salt in a heavy-bottomed saucepan. Add enough cold water to cover and bring to a boil over high heat. Reduce heat and simmer for 20 minutes, until potatoes are tender. Drain, then set aside to steam-dry for 3–5 minutes. Put potatoes through a potato ricer or mash until fluffy. Cover and set aside.

Heat coconut oil in a frying pan over medium-high heat, until nearly smoking. Reduce heat to medium, add cumin seeds, and sauté for 30 seconds, until lightly roasted. Add onion and ginger-garlic paste and cook for 7 minutes, until onions are softened and translucent.

Stir in coriander and chili powder and cook for 1 minute, until fragrant. Add spinach, increase heat to high, and sauté for 1 minute, or until wilted. Season with fenugreek, garam masala, and remaining ½ tsp salt.

Fold the spinach mixture into the mashed potatoes. Using your hands, form croquettes into 3-inch logs, about 1 inch in diameter.

In a clean bowl, beat eggs until smooth. Put breadcrumbs into a shallow dish. Dip a croquette cylinder into the egg, then carefully roll it in breadcrumbs. Place it onto a baking sheet and repeat with the remaining pieces.

Heat vegetable oil in a deep-fryer or deep saucepan over medium-high heat, until it reaches a temperature of 325°F. Carefully lower 2–3 croquettes into the oil (taking care not to splash) and deep-fry for 2 minutes, rolling them gently with a long-handled slotted spoon, until golden brown. Carefully transfer them to a plate lined with paper towels. Repeat with the remaining croquettes.

Serve immediately with chili-lime sauce.

MAKES 25

Parippu Vadas
പരിപ്പ് വട

This is an addictive little snack! Crispy, spicy, and protein-packed, parippu vadas are typically sold in coffee shops in south India and are traditionally served with a nice coffee or steaming cup of chai. Prepare a batch the next time you gather to watch the game—just be sure you leave a couple of hours for soaking the chana dal.

2 cups chana dal or yellow split peas, rinsed

1 onion, finely chopped

10–12 curry leaves, chopped

4 Indian or Thai green chiles, halved lengthwise

1 (½-inch) piece ginger, peeled and chopped

1½ tsp salt

½ tsp asafetida powder

½ tsp ground turmeric

2 cups vegetable oil, for deep-frying

To serve

Coconut Chutney (page 44) or Tomato Chutney (page 74)

Cardamom Chai (page 171)

IN A LARGE bowl, combine chana dal and 6 cups water and soak for 2 hours.

Drain well, then transfer lentils to a food processor and process into a coarse paste. Transfer paste to a clean bowl.

Add onions, curry leaves, chiles, ginger, salt, asafetida, and turmeric and mix well. Shape a spoon of the mixture into a 1-inch-diameter ball and, using the palm of your hand, slightly flatten. Repeat with the remaining mixture.

Heat the oil in a large frying pan over medium-high heat. Add patties (avoid overcrowding) and fry for 2 minutes. Flip over and fry for another 2 minutes, until golden brown. Transfer the vadas to a plate lined with paper towels. Repeat until all the vadas have been made.

Serve immediately with coconut or tomato chutney and cardamom chai.

MAKES 8

- 1 lb cooked king or snow crabmeat, drained and picked clean of shells
- 3 small shallots, finely chopped
- ½ green or red bell pepper, seeded, deveined, and finely chopped
- 20 curry leaves, coarsely chopped
- 3 Tbsp good-quality mayonnaise
- ¾ cup panko breadcrumbs
- 2 tsp Garam Masala (page 41)
- 2 tsp ground turmeric
- 1½ tsp coarsely ground black pepper
- 1½ tsp red chili powder
- 1 tsp ground cumin
- ½ tsp salt
- 1 Tbsp fresh lemon juice
- 2–3 Tbsp coconut oil
- Cilantro leaves, for garnish (optional)

To serve
- Vegetable Kuchumber (page 86)
- Chili-Lime Sauce (page 43) or garlic aioli

Crab Cakes
ക്രാബ് കേക്ക്

In order to irrigate fields and to transport crops, a network of lagoons and canals was carved into the Kerala countryside to connect the rivers, lakes, and inlets. The small crabs of this backwater area of Kerala (there are about twenty-seven species of crab) are the inspiration for our house crab cakes. We serve these with our Chili-Lime Sauce (page 43), but you can use any good garlicky aioli with a touch of citrus.

IN A LARGE bowl, combine well-squeezed crabmeat, shallots, bell peppers, curry leaves, and mayonnaise and mix well. Add breadcrumbs, garam masala, turmeric, pepper, chili powder, cumin, and salt and mix gently. Stir in lemon juice.

Shape a spoon of the mixture into a 2-inch-diameter ball and, using the palm of your hand, slightly flatten. Repeat with the remaining mixture.

Heat oil in a large frying pan over medium heat. Add the crab cakes (avoid overcrowding) and fry for 3 minutes. Flip over and fry for another 3 minutes, or until the cakes are golden brown. Transfer crab cakes to a plate lined with paper towels. Repeat with the remaining cakes, if necessary, making sure the oil is back to temperature before adding the next batch.

Garnish with cilantro (if using), and serve immediately with vegetable kuchumber and chili-lime sauce or aioli.

SERVES 4

Shrimp Kakkan
ചെമ്മീൻ കക്കാൻ

Kakkan means "chili-based" but this dish isn't super fiery, as one might think. The dominating spice, Kashmiri chili powder, is quite mild and used more for color and fragrance than fire. These are fantastic appetizers at a dinner party. Once marinated, the shrimp cook up in an instant.

IN A LARGE bowl, combine shrimp, ginger, yogurt, turmeric, and chili powder and mix well. Cover and refrigerate for 6 hours to marinate.

Heat oil in a large frying pan over medium-high heat. Add onion and curry leaves and sauté for 1 minute. Add shrimp mixture and sauté for another 1–2 minutes, until shrimp are just cooked. Season with salt, lime juice, and cilantro. Serve the hot shrimp on pappadums.

12 medium shrimp, peeled and deveined, with tails intact

1 (½-inch) piece ginger, peeled and cut into thin matchsticks

2 Tbsp plain yogurt

2 Tbsp ground turmeric

1½ tsp Kashmiri chili powder

3 Tbsp coconut oil

1 onion, thinly sliced

10 curry leaves

1½ tsp salt

1 Tbsp fresh lime juice

Handful of cilantro, chopped

To serve
Pappadums

SERVES 4

Scallops with Tomato Chutney
സ്കലൊപ്പ് വിത്ത് തക്കാളി ചട്നി

I tasted my first scallops in the Middle East, when I worked in the kitchens of the Oasis Resorts, and they made a lasting impression. These days, I buy succulent Digby scallops, and douse them with lime and a zesty spice blend before frying them up in coconut oil. They're wonderful on their own, but this vibrant tomato chutney—which can be prepared a day in advance—takes them to the next level.

Tomato chutney   Have a splash guard and measured spices nearby. Heat oil in a small frying pan over medium-high heat until nearly smoking. Immediately reduce heat to medium. (You can test the heat of the oil by dropping in a couple of seeds. The oil is at the correct temperature when the seeds crackle, but do not burn.) Add mustard seeds and temper for a few seconds, until they stop popping. (Cover with the splash guard, if needed.) Add chile pieces and curry leaves and cook for another 30 seconds until the leaves curl. Transfer the spices to a heavy-bottomed frying pan.

Working quickly, add onions and a pinch of salt and sauté for 30 seconds. Add chili powder and sauté for another 30 seconds. Stir in tomato purée and simmer for 5 minutes. Taste and adjust salt if needed.

Scallops   Using a mortar and pestle, or a spice grinder, combine chiles, black gram, fennel seeds, and peppercorns and grind into a coarse powder. Add turmeric and salt and mix well. Set aside on a plate.

Pat scallops dry, place in a bowl, and sprinkle with lime juice, then dredge them in the spice mix on both sides. Set aside on a clean plate.

Heat oil in a frying pan over medium-high heat, being careful not to let the oil smoke, or the spices will burn. Reduce heat to medium if necessary. Add scallops and sear for 1 minute, until a crust is formed. Turn them over and cook for 1 more minute.

Spoon the tomato chutney on top of each scallop and garnish with cilantro leaves.

Tomato chutney
1 Tbsp coconut oil
½ tsp black mustard seeds
1 dried red chile, snapped in half
8 curry leaves
1 onion, coarsely chopped
Pinch of salt, plus extra to taste
½ tsp red chili powder
2 small ripe tomatoes, puréed (1 cup)

Scallops
3 dried red chiles, snapped in half
1 Tbsp split and hulled black gram (*urad dal*)
1½ tsp fennel seeds
½ tsp black peppercorns
½ tsp ground turmeric
¼ tsp salt
12 medium scallops
1 Tbsp fresh lime juice
1 Tbsp coconut oil
Cilantro leaves, for garnish

To serve
Tomato Chutney (see here)

Tempering is a traditional method of extracting optimal flavor from Indian spices, and it is a skill learned with practice! Reducing the heat a little before adding the spices prevents the spices from burning and adding a bitterness to your dish. If they do burn, simply start again with fresh spices.

SERVES 4

Squid Peera
കണവ പീര

Peera means "grated coconut" and here the squid is simmered in a fragrant coconut paste made uniquely sour and slightly smoky with kudampuli (page 27). My mother would prepare this dish with sardines or anchovies. Here, we've used squid, but you could also use shrimp or scallops.

4 kudampuli (Malabar tamarind)

10 small shallots, thinly sliced

2 cloves garlic, chopped

1 cup fresh or frozen grated coconut

½ tsp ground turmeric

2 Tbsp coconut oil (divided)

10 curry leaves

4 Indian or Thai green chiles, halved lengthwise

1 (½-inch) piece ginger, cut into thin matchsticks

1 lb squid, cleaned and cut into rings

IN A SMALL bowl, combine kudampuli and ¼ cup warm water (or just enough to cover) and set aside for 15–20 minutes to soften. If the pieces are large, cut them into 2–3 smaller pieces, then return to soaking water. Set aside.

In a food processor, combine shallots, garlic, coconut, and turmeric and process to a coarse paste. Set aside.

Drain the kudampuli, reserving the soaking water. Heat 1 Tbsp oil in a large frying pan over medium heat. Add curry leaves, chiles, ginger, kudampuli, and the shallot-coconut paste and sauté for 2 minutes, until fragrant.

Add squid and 1 Tbsp of reserved soaking water and simmer over medium-high heat for 4–5 minutes, until the squid is cooked through.

Transfer the squid peera to a serving platter. Heat the remaining 1 Tbsp coconut oil in the same pan, then drizzle it over the dish. Serve.

SERVES 6

Tamarind paste

3–4 oz tamarind pulp, broken into small chunks

Lamb chops

6 small lamb chops, frenched

2 Tbsp Ginger-Garlic Paste (page 42)

2 tsp fresh lemon juice

¼ cup plain yogurt

½ tsp salt

1 tsp Garam Masala (page 41), plus extra for finishing

1 tsp red chili powder

¼ tsp ground turmeric

¼ tsp coriander seeds

1 tsp coarsely ground black pepper

2 Tbsp Tamarind Paste (see here)

10 curry leaves, chopped (divided)

1 Tbsp coconut oil

Mint, for garnish

To serve

Mint Chutney (page 45)

1 lime, cut into wedges

Kerala Lamb Chops

കേരള ലാമ്പ് ചോപ്സ്

The key to these luscious chops is the marinating of the meat—so don't eliminate that all-important step! The longer the lamb sits in the ginger-garlic-lemon paste, the more tender and flavorful it will be. The lamb chops are "frenched," which means that some of the meat and sinew is scraped off part of the bone for a cleaner look. (You can ask your butcher to do this for you.)

Tamarind paste Place tamarind in a small bowl, add enough boiling water to cover, and set aside for 20–30 minutes to soften. Transfer softened pulp to a fine-mesh strainer set over a clean bowl. Using a spoon or spatula, push the pulp through the strainer to separate the tamarind paste from its fibers (and occasional seeds). Scrape the paste from the underside of the strainer to collect as much as you can. Discard the fibers and set the paste aside.

Lamb chops In a large bowl, combine lamb chops, ginger-garlic paste, and lemon juice. Cover and refrigerate for 4–6 hours.

In another large bowl, combine yogurt, salt, garam masala, chili powder, turmeric, coriander, pepper, tamarind paste, and half the chopped curry leaves and blend into a paste.

Transfer the lamb chops to the bowl of spiced yogurt, and mix to coat them well. Cover bowl and refrigerate for another 6 hours.

Heat oil in a large frying pan over medium-high heat. Brush excess yogurt off lamb chops and add the chops to the pan. Cook for 4 minutes, flip over, then cook for another 3 minutes. Add the remaining chopped curry leaves, toss, and cook for 1 more minute to toast them a little. (The lamb chops will be medium-rare). Set the chops aside to rest for 5 minutes.

Season lamb chops with a pinch of garam masala and mint leaves and serve with mint chutney and lime wedges.

83 **Kerala-Style Slaw**

84 **Black Chickpea Salad**

86 **Vegetable Kuchumber**

87 **Cabbage Thoran**

89 **Broccoli Thoran**

90 **Mezhukkupuratti**

93 **Carrot and Coconut Foogath**

94 **Pumpkin Erissery**

97 **Kerala-Style Vegetable Stew**

98 **Nadan Vegetable Korma**

100 **Mushroom Aviyal**

101 **Potato Masala**

102 **Cauliflower Masala**

105 **Baby Eggplant Masala**

107 **Dal Masala**

108 **Egg Mappas**

109 **Chickpea Curry**

110 **Mango Curry**

113 **Ooty Mushroom Curry**

114 **Masoor Dal and Spinach Curry**

Onam sadya

Onam is Kerala's Thanksgiving and New Year's in one—a ten-day carnival of flowers, art, song, dance, sport, and spectacle, celebrated by Malayalis around the world. There are many elements to Onam, but the one loved above all is the traditional feast. Called the *sadya*, which means "banquet" in our Malayalam language, it's a cornucopia of the finest food harvested from the land.

We were keen to introduce Ottawa to this important part of our heritage so we hosted our first Onam sadya in our first year. Fifteen years later, it's become one of the most important dates in the Coconut Lagoon calendar, with the afternoon sadya sold out months ahead.

This multi-course vegetarian spread includes rice, rasam, yogurt, various curries, pappadums, plantain chips, pickles, chutneys, and even sambaram, to help settle the tummy. It is always served in a particular order, from left to right, on a fresh banana leaf. The leaf is the plate, red matta rice is the anchor, then comes the bounty—dollops of this, piles of that, and scoops of hot curry—which keeps coming and coming, until you indicate you are sated by folding the leaf away from you. And often wishing you'd done that a while ago.

1. Raw banana
2. Sarkara varatti (banana chips with jaggery)
3. Banana chips
4. Dried red chiles
5. Pappadum
6. Salt
7. Beet pachadi
8. Pumpkin erissery (page 94)
9. Curried yogurt (*puliserry*)
10. Sambaram (page 168)
11. Semiya payasam (page 175)
12. Rasam
13. Baby eggplant masala (page 105)
14. Vegetable stew (page 97)
15. Matta rice (page 157)
16. Ghee (page 41)
17. Dal masala (page 107)
18. Aviyal (mushroom version in book)(page 100)
19. Pineapple pachadi (page 46)
20. Cabbage thoran (page 87)
21. Sambar
22. Ginger pickle
23. Lemon and date pickle (page 51)
24. Mango pickle (page 50)

SERVES 4

2 cups finely shredded green cabbage

3 carrots, shredded (1½ cups)

¼ green bell pepper, finely chopped

1 Indian or Thai green chile, sliced lengthwise into slivers

2 Tbsp vegetable oil

1½ Tbsp coconut vinegar

1 tsp coarsely ground black pepper

1 tsp salt

Kerala-Style Slaw

കേരള-സ്റ്റൈൽ സ്ലോ

This refreshing salad is the perfect accompaniment to grilled meats and fish on a warm summer day. Coconut vinegar lends this simple slaw a true Kerala kick, but in a pinch, white vinegar will do.

IN A LARGE bowl, combine cabbage, carrots, bell peppers, and chile slivers. In a separate small bowl, combine the oil, vinegar, black pepper, and salt.

Add the dressing to the salad bowl and mix well. Serve chilled.

1 cup dried black chickpeas, rinsed and soaked overnight

1 red onion, finely chopped

1–2 carrots, finely chopped

½ green bell pepper, seeded, deveined, and finely chopped

1½ Tbsp fresh lemon juice

1½ Tbsp vegetable oil

½ tsp salt

¼ tsp red chili powder

1 tsp cumin powder

Curry leaves, for garnish

Cilantro leaves, for garnish

SERVES 6–8

Black Chickpea Salad
ബ്ലാക്ക് ചിക്പീ സാലഡ്

In Kerala, the black chickpea (*kala chana*) is very common and, in my opinion, far tastier than the traditional white chickpea. Smaller and more intensely flavored than their white cousins, they are often used in a classic breakfast curry that is slow-cooked and has a thick coconut gravy. Here, they're found in a tasty, healthy salad, perfect for a summer gathering. You'll need to soak the chickpeas overnight before cooking them.

DRAIN CHICKPEAS. PUT chickpeas into a large saucepan, add 8 cups salted water, and bring to a boil. Reduce heat to a simmer and cook for 1 hour, until tender. Drain, then set aside to cool.

In a large bowl, combine all the ingredients and mix well. Garnish with cilantro and curry leaves and serve.

SERVES 4

1 tomato

1 carrot, finely chopped

1 red onion, finely chopped

1 small cucumber, finely chopped (1 cup)

½ cup finely shredded green cabbage

½ green bell pepper, seeded, deveined, and cut into matchsticks

15 curry leaves

2 Indian or Thai green chiles, cut into thin strips

Small bunch of cilantro, coarsely chopped

½ tsp sugar

½ tsp salt

½ tsp coarsely ground black pepper

½ tsp chaat masala

2 Tbsp vegetable oil

2 tsp fresh lime juice

Sliced cucumber, for garnish

Vegetable Kuchumber

വെജിറ്റബിൾ കുച്ചുമ്പർ

There aren't many salads in our cuisine, and those we have tend to be simple assemblies like this one, of fresh crunchy vegetables seasoned with cilantro, green chiles, and curry leaves, and brightened with lime. Crisp and refreshing, it's the ideal summer barbecue salad.

BRING A SMALL saucepan of water to a boil. Score an "x" on the bottom of the tomato, add it to the water, and boil for 30 seconds. Drain, then plunge the tomato into a bowl of ice water. Once it cools, peel off skin, cut in half, then remove seeds and cut into thin strips.

In a large bowl, combine all the vegetables. Add curry leaves, chiles, cilantro, sugar, salt, pepper, chaat masala, oil, and lime juice and mix well.

Adjust seasoning if needed and garnish with cucumber slices.

SERVES 6 (AS A SIDE DISH)

Cabbage Thoran

ക്യാബേജ് തോരൻ

Every Kerala meal will have at least one *thoran*, a dry dish similar to a Chinese stir-fry. I recommend you buy firm, green cabbage and shred it as evenly as possible. Here, we've combined cabbage with carrot and chiles, but you can adjust it to preference. This dish can also be served cold as a salad.

IN A BOWL, combine cabbage, carrot, and turmeric and mix well. Set aside.

Have a splash guard and measured spices nearby. Heat oil in a small frying pan over medium-high heat until nearly smoking. Immediately reduce the heat to medium. (You can test the heat of the oil by dropping in a couple of seeds. The oil is at the correct temperature when the seeds crackle, but do not burn.) Add mustard seeds and temper for a few seconds, until they stop popping. (Cover with the splash guard, if needed.) Immediately add black gram, chiles, and curry leaves and sauté for 2–3 minutes, until the black gram turns golden brown.

Add onions and sauté for 7 minutes, until softened and translucent. Increase heat to high. Add the cabbage and carrot mixture and cook, stirring constantly, until cabbage and carrot are soft and liquid has evaporated.

Stir in grated coconut and salt and cook for 1 more minute. Taste and adjust seasoning, if needed. Serve warm.

- 1 cup shredded green cabbage
- ½ carrot, shredded or finely chopped
- ¼ tsp ground turmeric
- 1½ Tbsp coconut oil
- 1½ tsp black mustard seeds
- 1½ tsp split and hulled black gram (*urad dal*)
- 2 dried red chiles, snapped in half
- 8–10 curry leaves, coarsely chopped
- 1 onion, coarsely chopped (½ cup)
- ½ cup fresh or frozen grated coconut
- ½ tsp salt

Tempering is a traditional method of extracting optimal flavor from Indian spices, and it is a skill learned with practice! Reducing the heat a little before adding the spices prevents the spices from burning and adding a bitterness to your dish. If they do burn, simply start again with fresh spices.

SERVES 4

Broccoli Thoran
ബ്രോക്കോലി തോരൻ

Vitamin-packed broccoli is a kitchen staple, and this quick and simple midweek dish is perfect for those looking for new inspiration. A one-pan supper, it is packed with flavor from the tempered spices and grated coconut. Make sure not to overcook the broccoli spears, though—they need to maintain a little crunch—and feel free to modify the number of chiles to suit your palate.

HAVE A SPLASH guard and measured spices nearby. Heat oil in a small frying pan over medium-high heat until nearly smoking. Immediately reduce heat to medium. (You can test the heat of the oil by dropping in a couple of seeds. The oil is at the correct temperature when the seeds crackle, but do not burn.) Add mustard seeds and temper for a few seconds, until they stop popping. (Cover with the splash guard, if needed.) Add red chiles and curry leaves and cook for a few more seconds. Transfer the spices to a large heavy-bottomed skillet.

Add onions and sauté for 7 minutes, until softened and translucent. Add coconut, turmeric, green chiles, and salt and stir. Add broccoli, mix well, and cook for 3 minutes, until the broccoli is al dente.

Serve with rice.

1 Tbsp coconut oil

1 tsp black mustard seeds

4 dried red chiles, snapped in half

4–6 curry leaves

1 large onion, chopped (1 cup)

⅓ cup fresh or frozen grated coconut

½ tsp ground turmeric

2–3 Indian or Thai green chiles, finely chopped

Salt, to taste

3 cups finely chopped broccoli spears

To serve
Basmati Rice (page 156)

Tempering is a traditional method of extracting optimal flavor from Indian spices, and it is a skill learned with practice! Reducing the heat a little before adding the spices prevents the spices from burning and adding a bitterness to your dish. If they do burn, simply start again with fresh spices.

- 12 tindoras or baby zucchini, quartered lengthwise (2 cups)
- 3 unripe bananas or plantains, unpeeled and washed, cut into 3-inch batons (2 cups)
- 4–6 Indian or Thai green chiles, halved lengthwise
- 1 tsp salt
- ½ tsp ground turmeric
- 1 Tbsp coconut oil
- 1½ tsp black mustard seeds
- ½ cup thinly sliced shallots
- 4 curry leaves, coarsely chopped
- 4 cloves garlic, crushed
- 2 dried red chiles, snapped in pieces

To serve
Basmati Rice (page 156)

> **Tempering** is a traditional method of extracting optimal flavor from Indian spices, and it is a skill learned with practice! Reducing the heat a little before adding the spices prevents the spices from burning and adding a bitterness to your dish. If they do burn, simply start again with fresh spices.

DF GF VG

SERVES 4

Mezhukkupuratti
മെഴുകുപുരട്ടി

Mezhukkupuratti is a traditional south Indian dish of stir-fried vegetables elevated with warm, fragrant spices. Prepared with green bananas or plantains (with the skin left on!), this simple dish makes an excellent side for any good meat curry, such as Beef Curry (page 146). Tindora, also known as ivy gourd or *kovakka*, is a tropical vine that grows abundantly in Kerala. If tindoras are unavailable, baby zucchini can be substituted.

IN A MEDIUM saucepan, combine tindoras (or baby zucchini), bananas (or plantains), green chiles, salt, and turmeric, and add 2½ cups water. Bring to a boil, reduce heat, and simmer for 5 minutes, until softened. Drain and set aside to steam-dry.

Have a splash guard and measured spices nearby. Heat oil in a small frying pan over medium-high heat until nearly smoking. Immediately reduce heat to medium. (You can test the heat of the oil by dropping in a couple of seeds. The oil is at the correct temperature when the seeds crackle, but do not burn.) Add mustard seeds and temper for a few seconds, until they stop popping. (Cover with the splash guard, if needed.) Transfer the mustard seeds to a large heavy-bottomed skillet.

Immediately add shallots, curry leaves, garlic, and red chiles and sauté for 2 minutes, until shallots have softened. Add the vegetables and mix well.

Serve warm with rice.

SERVES 8 (AS A SIDE DISH)

2 Tbsp coconut oil

2 dried red chiles, snapped in half

1½ Tbsp cumin seeds

1 Tbsp split and hulled black gram (*urad dal*)

10 curry leaves

2 small onions, finely chopped

4–6 carrots, shredded (2 cups)

½ cup fresh or frozen grated coconut

1 tsp salt

To serve

Basmati Rice (page 156)

Carrot and Coconut Foogath

കാരറ്റ് തേങ്ങ ഫുഗാത്

Foogath comes from the Portuguese word *refogar*, which means "to sauté." This Goan side dish is light, versatile, and quick to prepare and can be made with any number of vegetables—cabbage, carrots, green beans, yard-long beans, or cauliflower. We use a traditional uruli at Coconut Lagoon, but a flat-bottomed wok or wide frying pan works well.

HEAT OIL IN a wok or a small frying pan over medium-high heat until nearly smoking. Reduce heat to medium. Add chiles, cumin, black gram, and curry leaves and sauté for 1–2 minutes, until lightly brown and fragrant. Add onions, increase heat to medium-high, and sauté for 1 minute.

Add carrots, coconut, and salt and sauté for 2–3 minutes, until softened.

Serve with rice.

1 cup dried adzuki beans (red cowpeas), soaked overnight

3½ tsp salt (divided)

1 lb butternut squash or pumpkin, peeled, seeded, and cut into ½-inch cubes

3–5 Indian or Thai green chiles, halved lengthwise, plus extra for garnish

Pinch of ground turmeric

2 Tbsp chopped ginger

1 cup fresh or frozen grated coconut

½ tsp cumin seeds

¼ cup coconut oil

1 tsp mustard seeds

20 curry leaves, plus extra for garnish

To serve
Basmati Rice (page 156)

> **Tempering** is a traditional method of extracting optimal flavor from Indian spices, and it is a skill learned with practice! Reducing the heat a little before adding the spices prevents the spices from burning and adding a bitterness to your dish. If they do burn, simply start again with fresh spices.

Pumpkin Erissery

മത്തങ്ങ എരിശ്ശേരി

Erissery means "paired together" and the dish is an essential part of a sadya (page 80). Here, we've paired butternut squash with adzuki beans, though traditionally this hearty dish would be prepared with the thick-fleshed pumpkins we grow in Kerala. Substitute with other varieties of pumpkin and squash when available in the fall.

DF GF VG

SERVES 4

BRING A SAUCEPAN of water to a boil, add beans and 3 tsp salt, and cook for 15–20 minutes, or until softened. Drain and set aside.

In a large saucepan, combine squash (or pumpkin) with chiles, ginger, turmeric, the remaining ½ tsp salt, and enough water just to cover. Bring to a boil, reduce heat, and simmer for 10–15 minutes, until the squash is very soft and almost dry.

Using a mini food processor or a mortar and pestle, combine coconut and cumin seeds and pound into a smooth paste. Add half the paste to the squash mixture. Add the beans and mix well.

Have a splash guard and measured spices nearby. Heat oil in a small frying pan over medium-high heat until nearly smoking. Immediately reduce heat to medium. (You can test the heat of the oil by dropping in a couple of seeds. The oil is at the correct temperature when the seeds crackle, but do not burn.) Add mustard seeds and temper for a few seconds, until they stop popping. (Cover with the splash guard, if needed.) Add curry leaves and remaining coconut-cumin paste and cook for 1–2 minutes, until the coconut begins to brown.

Transfer this mixture to the pumpkin erissery and stir well. Garnish with curry leaves and chiles. Serve with rice.

SERVES 4

Kerala-Style Vegetable Stew
കേരള-സ്റ്റൈൽ വെജിറ്റബിൾ സ്റ്റൂ

This rustic stew is packed with tender vegetables and flavored with whole-roasted spices, giving it a real taste of comfort. Feel free to mix up the vegetables—and for an extra treat, garnish with fried onions, cashews, and raisins.

Vegetable stew Heat oil in a large, heavy-bottomed saucepan over medium heat. Add cinnamon, cardamom, cloves, and star anise and roast for 1–2 minutes, until fragrant. Add chiles, ginger, garlic, and curry leaves and sauté for 1 minute.

Add onions and salt and sauté for 3 minutes, until just softened. Stir in potatoes and carrots. Pour in coconut milk and ½ cup water, cover, and bring to a boil. Reduce heat and simmer for 6 minutes, until vegetables are softened. Add cauliflower, beans, and peas and simmer for 2 minutes until just cooked.

Garnish Heat ghee in a small frying pan over medium-high heat, add cashews and raisins, and sauté for 1 minute. Set aside.

Assembly Sprinkle black pepper and fried onions on top of the stew. Add the cashews and raisins (if using) and serve with appam.

Vegetable stew

½ cup coconut oil

1–2 sticks cinnamon, roughly cracked

10 green cardamom pods

10 cloves

1 star anise

5 Indian or Thai green chiles, halved lengthwise

1 (½-inch) piece ginger, peeled and cut into thin matchsticks

4 cloves garlic, thinly sliced

20 curry leaves

1 onion, coarsely chopped

1 tsp salt

1 large potato, cut into ½-inch cubes

1 carrot, cut into ½-inch cubes

2 cups coconut milk

1 cup cauliflower florets

½ cup chopped green beans, cut into ½-inch segments

½ cup fresh or frozen peas

1 tsp coarsely ground black pepper

Fried Onions (page 42), for garnish

Garnish (optional)

2 Tbsp Ghee (page 41)

Handful of raw cashew nuts

Handful of raisins

To serve

Appam (page 54)

Earth   97

¼ cup coconut oil

1 tsp cumin seeds

1 large onion, chopped (1 cup)

3 cloves garlic, finely chopped

2–4 Indian or Thai green chiles, chopped

2 potatoes, cut into ½-inch cubes

1 carrot, cut into ½-inch cubes

1 Tbsp ground turmeric

2 tsp salt, plus extra to taste

4 cups coconut milk (divided)

1 cup cauliflower florets

½ cup chopped green beans, cut into 1-inch segments

½ cup fresh or frozen peas

Pinch of Garam Masala (page 41)

2 Tbsp Fried Onions (page 42), for garnish (optional)

To serve
Malabar Parathas (page 60)

SERVES 4

Nadan Vegetable Korma
നാടൻ വെജിറ്റബിൾ കുറുമ

A korma (or kurma) is a thick, seasonal stew, fairly sweet and easily made. While korma is made with cream in northern India, we use coconut milk (of course) in Kerala and typically serve it with chewy parathas (page 60). You could also serve this with any rice from the rice chapter (pages 154–62). Feel free to mix up the vegetables based on what's available in the garden, the market, or the fridge.

HEAT OIL IN a heavy-bottomed frying pan over medium-high heat, until nearly smoking. Reduce heat to medium, add cumin, and sauté for 30 seconds, until fragrant. Add onions and sauté for 7 minutes, until softened and translucent. Add garlic and chiles and sauté for 1 more minute.

Stir in potatoes, carrots, turmeric, and salt. Pour in 2 cups coconut milk and 1 cup water and boil for 10 minutes, until gravy has thickened and vegetables have softened. Add cauliflower, beans, and peas and cook for 2–3 minutes, until softened.

Pour in the remaining 2 cups coconut milk and bring to a boil, then remove from heat. Season with salt to taste. Add garam masala and set aside for 10–15 minutes to rest.

Scatter fried onions on top (if using) and serve with parathas.

Tamarind paste

8 oz tamarind pulp, broken into small chunks

Mushroom aviyal

10 curry leaves

10 shallots

1 Indian or Thai green chile

1 cup fresh or frozen grated coconut

¼ cup Tamarind Paste (see here)

1 Tbsp cumin seeds

½ tsp ground turmeric

1 Tbsp coconut oil

4 cups assorted mushrooms, cleaned and thinly sliced

1 tsp salt

To serve

Basmati Rice (page 156)

Mushroom Aviyal

കൂണ് അവിയൽ

When we were kids in Kerala, my mother would send me or a brother to the market with two rupees to buy vegetables for the evening's aviyal, a thick and hearty vegetable stew, and a dish essential to the vegetarian feast of Onam. For this recipe, we've used a mix of Ontario mushrooms, both wild and cultivated, but you can use the straight button variety if that's what's available.

Tamarind paste Place tamarind in a small bowl, add enough boiling water to cover, and set aside for 20–30 minutes to soften. Transfer softened pulp to a fine-mesh strainer set over a clean bowl. Using a spoon or spatula, push the pulp through the strainer to separate the tamarind paste from its fibers (and occasional seeds). Scrape the paste from the underside of the strainer to collect as much as you can. Discard the fibers and set the paste aside.

Mushroom aviyal In a food processor, combine curry leaves, shallots, chile, coconut, tamarind paste, cumin, and turmeric and blend into a smooth paste.

Heat oil in a frying pan over high heat. Add mushrooms and sauté for 1–2 minutes, until wilted. Stir in the coconut mixture and cook until all liquid has evaporated. Season with salt.

Serve with rice.

SERVES 4

Potato Masala

ഉരുളക്കിഴങ്ങ് മസാല

Masala is a Hindi word for "spice" or "spices." It can refer as well to a mix of spices—such as a garam masala or chaat masala—and to the dish itself, which features a particular blend of spices within a sauce. In this dish, we've taken the humble potato and given it a spice kick! Enormously versatile, it is the traditional stuffing for a dosa (page 56) but it pairs very well with pretty much any dish—a nice rare steak, lamb chops, or a chicken or fish curry. The hulled black gram (*urad dal*) also lends a lovely crunch.

PUT POTATOES, TURMERIC, and 2 tsp salt in a large saucepan. Add enough cold water to cover the potatoes by an inch. Bring to a boil, reduce heat, and simmer for 20 minutes, until potatoes are tender. Drain, then mash. Set aside.

Have a splash guard and measured spices nearby. Heat oil in a small frying pan over medium-high heat until nearly smoking. Immediately reduce heat to medium. (You can test the heat of the oil by dropping in a couple of seeds. The oil is at the correct temperature when the seeds crackle, but do not burn.) Add mustard seeds and temper for a few seconds, until they stop popping. (Cover with the splash guard, if needed.) Add black gram, red chiles, and curry leaves and cook for another few seconds until black gram begins to turn brown. Add ginger and garlic and sauté for 1–2 minutes, until lightly brown and fragrant. Transfer to a large heavy-bottomed skillet.

Add onions, green chiles, and remaining 1 tsp salt and sauté over medium heat for 2–3 minutes, until onions have softened. Add carrots and sauté for 1 minute. Add mashed potato and mix well. Pour in milk and add ghee, then adjust salt to taste.

Garnish with curry leaves and cilantro (if using).

---

2 lbs yellow potatoes, such as Yukon Gold (about 6–8), peeled and coarsely chopped

1½ tsp ground turmeric

3 tsp salt, plus extra to taste (divided)

¼ cup coconut oil

1½ tsp black mustard seeds

1½ tsp split and hulled black gram (*urad dal*)

2 dried red chiles, snapped in half

15 curry leaves, plus extra for garnish

2 Tbsp finely chopped ginger

3 cloves garlic, thinly sliced

2 onions, thinly sliced

2–4 Indian or Thai green chiles, halved lengthwise

¼ cup finely sliced carrots

1 cup milk

1 Tbsp Ghee (page 41)

Coarsely chopped cilantro, for garnish (optional)

Tempering is a traditional method of extracting optimal flavor from Indian spices, and it is a skill learned with practice! Reducing the heat a little before adding the spices prevents the spices from burning and adding a bitterness to your dish. If they do burn, simply start again with fresh spices.

Earth

1 yellow potato, such as Yukon Gold, peeled and cut into ½-inch cubes

½ tsp ground turmeric

½ tsp salt

1 head cauliflower, cut into florets

2 Tbsp coconut oil

15 curry leaves, plus extra for garnish

1½ tsp cumin seeds

2 onions, cut into large chunks

1 Tbsp Ginger-Garlic Paste (page 42)

2 Indian or Thai green chiles, finely chopped

1 Tbsp ground coriander

1 tsp Garam Masala (page 41), plus extra for sprinkling

1 tsp red chili powder

3 large ripe tomatoes, chopped

1½ tsp fresh lime juice

Cilantro and lime slices, for garnish

To serve
Basmati Rice (page 156)

Cauliflower Masala

ക്വാളിഫ്ലവർ മസാല

During my high school years, my father took a job in Bangalore in the state of Karnataka. Every three weeks, he'd take the overnight bus home to Thrissur, with a couple of cauliflowers (*gobhee*) in his bag, and my mother would prepare this dish for dinner—spinning out the precious treats from the hills of Karnataka with potato and tomato.

BRING A LARGE saucepan of water to a boil over high heat. Add potatoes, turmeric, and salt and boil for 12 minutes, or until soft but not yielding. Add cauliflower and cook for another 3–4 minutes. (Potato and cauliflower should be cooked, but still firm.) Drain and set aside.

Heat oil in a wok or large frying pan over medium heat. Add curry leaves and cumin and cook for 20–30 seconds, until fragrant. Add onions, ginger-garlic paste, and chiles and sauté them 1–2 minutes, or until the raw smell is cooked off. Stir in coriander, garam masala, and chili powder and cook for 1 minute. Add tomatoes and cook for another 3 minutes. Stir in potato and cauliflower masala. Finish with lime juice and a sprinkle of garam masala.

Transfer to a serving bowl. Garnish with curry leaves, cilantro, and lime slices and serve with rice.

SERVES 4

Baby Eggplant Masala
വഴുതനങ്ങ മസാല

This simple dish sees small, teardrop-shaped Indian eggplants infused with ginger-garlic paste and warmed with tempered spices and curry leaves. The eggplants are roasted until softened, then tossed into a fragrant tomato sauce that's finished with tamarind.

Tamarind paste Place tamarind in a small bowl, add enough boiling water to cover, and set aside for 20–30 minutes to soften. Transfer softened pulp to a fine-mesh strainer set over a clean bowl. Using a spoon or spatula, push the pulp through the strainer to separate the tamarind paste from its fibers (and occasional seeds). Scrape the paste from the underside of the strainer to collect as much as you can. Discard the fibers and set the paste aside.

Baby eggplant masala Preheat oven to 375°F.

Lightly score the flesh of the eggplants and season with ½ tsp salt. Place them on a baking sheet and bake for 20 minutes, or until just tender.

Have a splash guard and measured spices nearby. Heat oil in a small frying pan over medium-high heat until nearly smoking. Immediately reduce heat to medium. (You can test the heat of the oil by dropping in a couple of seeds. The oil is at the correct temperature when the seeds crackle, but do not burn.) Add mustard seeds and temper for a few seconds, until they stop popping. (Cover with the splash guard, if needed.) Add fenugreek seeds and curry leaves and cook for a few more seconds. Transfer the spices to a large heavy-bottomed skillet.

Add onions and the remaining ½ tsp salt and sauté over medium heat for 1 minute. Stir in ginger-garlic paste and cook for another 2 minutes until lightly brown and fragrant. Stir in tomatoes and cook for 3 minutes, until softened. Add coriander, chili powder, and turmeric and stir for 1 minute. Stir in tamarind paste, increase heat, and cook until mixture starts to bubble. Add eggplants, reduce heat, and simmer gently for 5 minutes.

Garnish with curry leaves. Serve warm with rice or parathas.

Tamarind paste
3–4 oz tamarind pulp, broken into small chunks

Baby eggplant masala
8 small Indian or baby eggplants, halved lengthwise

1 tsp salt (divided)

1 Tbsp coconut oil

1½ tsp black mustard seeds

½ tsp fenugreek seeds

10 curry leaves, plus extra for garnish

2 onions, coarsely chopped

1 Tbsp Ginger-Garlic Paste (page 42)

2 large tomatoes, coarsely chopped

1 Tbsp ground coriander

1 tsp red chili powder

½ tsp ground turmeric

2 Tbsp Tamarind Paste (see here)

To serve
Lemon Rice (page 160), Curd Rice (page 161), or Malabar Parathas (page 60)

> **Tempering** is a traditional method of extracting optimal flavor from Indian spices, and it is a skill learned with practice! Reducing the heat a little before adding the spices prevents the spices from burning and adding a bitterness to your dish. If they do burn, simply start again with fresh spices.

Earth

SERVES 4

Dal Masala
പരിപ്പ് മസാല

Dal masala means "day off" to me, and this dish is part of my Tuesday family dinners with Suma, Marieann, Mathew, and Michael. This quick-cooked comfort dish is typically served with Matta Rice (page 157) and Kerala Raita (page 43).

2 cups dried red lentils, rinsed

½ tsp salt, plus extra to taste

1 tsp ground turmeric (divided)

¼ cup coconut oil

1½ tsp black mustard seeds

1 tsp cumin seeds

4 dried red chiles, snapped in half

15 whole curry leaves

2½ onions, finely chopped (1½ cups)

3 cloves garlic, finely chopped

½ tsp red chili powder

1 large ripe tomato, chopped

Juice of ½ lemon

Fresh cilantro leaves, coarsely chopped, for garnish

To serve
Basmati Rice (page 156)

IN A HEAVY-BOTTOMED saucepan, combine lentils, salt, and ½ tsp turmeric. Pour in 4 cups water and bring to a boil over high heat. Reduce heat and simmer uncovered for 12–15 minutes, or until lentils have softened. Set aside.

Have a splash guard and measured spices nearby. Heat oil in a small frying pan over medium-high heat until nearly smoking. Immediately reduce heat to medium. (You can test the heat of the oil by dropping in a couple of seeds. The oil is at the correct temperature when the seeds crackle, but do not burn.) Add mustard seeds and temper for a few seconds, until they stop popping. (Cover with the splash guard, if needed.) Add cumin, chiles, and curry leaves and sauté for another 10–15 seconds. Transfer the spices to a large heavy-bottomed skillet.

Add onions and sweat over medium heat for 7 minutes, until softened and translucent. Add garlic and sauté for 1 minute.

Add remaining ½ tsp turmeric and chili powder and stir well, taking care not to burn. (Reduce heat if necessary.) Add tomatoes and cook for 3 minutes. Stir in lentils and add a little water to loosen the curry. Bring to a boil, season with salt to taste, and add lemon juice.

Garnish with cilantro and serve with rice.

> **Tempering** is a traditional method of extracting optimal flavor from Indian spices, and it is a skill learned with practice! Reducing the heat a little before adding the spices prevents the spices from burning and adding a bitterness to your dish. If they do burn, simply start again with fresh spices.

Earth

2½ Tbsp coconut oil

1½ tsp fennel seeds

2–4 Indian or Thai green chiles

15 curry leaves

1 Tbsp Ginger-Garlic Paste (page 42)

2 large onions, chopped (3 cups)

1 tsp salt

2 tsp ground turmeric

1 cup coconut milk

Pinch of coarsely ground black pepper

Pinch of ground cumin

8 hard-boiled eggs, halved lengthwise

SERVES 4

Egg Mappas
എഗ്ഗ് മപ്പാസ്

Kerala-style eggs are wildly popular on our brunch menu. Mappas is a rich, coconut milk–based dish, particularly popular with the Syrian-Christian community. Here, hard-boiled eggs are added to the heady, aromatic gravy.

HEAT OIL IN a large frying pan over high heat, until nearly smoking. Reduce the heat to medium, add fennel seeds, and sauté for 30 seconds. Add chiles, curry leaves, and ginger-garlic paste and sauté for 2–3 minutes, until fragrant.

Add onions and salt and sweat over medium heat for 7 minutes, until softened and translucent. Stir in turmeric and cook for 1 minute, until the raw smell is cooked off.

Stir in coconut milk, pepper, and cumin and cook over medium-high heat for 2 minutes. Adjust seasoning to taste.

Transfer eggs to a bowl or platter. Pour sauce carefully over eggs and serve immediately.

SERVES 4–6

Chickpea Curry

വെള്ള കടല കറി

Typically considered a north Indian dish (*chana masala*), our version uses cumin, curry leaves, and coconut milk. The secret to success with this curry is in the preparation and cooking of the chickpeas. I prefer dried chickpeas—they don't have a tinny flavor, their texture can be controlled through cooking, and they're more economical.

DRAIN CHICKPEAS. In a large heavy-bottomed saucepan, combine chickpeas and 8 cups of salted water. Bring to a boil over high heat, then reduce to low, cover, and simmer for 1 hour or until the chickpeas are cooked through. Drain and set aside. (Makes 2½ cups.)

Have a splash guard and measured spices nearby. Heat oil in a small frying pan over medium-high heat until nearly smoking. Immediately reduce heat to medium. (You can test the heat of the oil by dropping in a couple of seeds. The oil is at the correct temperature when the seeds crackle, but do not burn.) Add mustard seeds and temper for a few seconds, until they stop popping. (Cover with the splash guard, if needed.) Add cumin and curry leaves and cook for another few seconds. Transfer the spices to a large heavy-bottomed skillet.

Add onions, garlic, ginger, chiles, and salt and sauté over medium heat for 7 minutes, or until onions are softened. Add coriander, turmeric, and chili powder and cook for 1 minute. Stir in tomatoes and simmer gently for 5 minutes.

Pour in coconut milk, stir in chickpeas, and bring to a boil, stirring continuously. Reduce heat and simmer for 5 minutes, until spices infuse chickpeas. Finish with a sprinkle of garam masala. Ladle curry over rice and serve.

---

1 cup dried chickpeas, soaked overnight in 3 cups of lightly salted water

¼ cup coconut oil

1 tsp black mustard seeds

1 tsp cumin seeds

10 curry leaves

1 large onion, chopped (1 cup)

3 cloves garlic, thinly sliced

1 (2-inch) piece ginger, peeled and chopped

6 Indian or Thai green chiles, halved lengthwise

1½ tsp salt

2 tsp ground coriander

2 tsp ground turmeric

1½ tsp red chili powder

1 large ripe tomato, finely chopped

1 cup coconut milk

Garam Masala (page 41), for sprinkling

To serve

Basmati Rice (page 156)

Tempering is a traditional method of extracting optimal flavor from Indian spices, and it is a skill learned with practice! Reducing the heat a little before adding the spices prevents the spices from burning and adding a bitterness to your dish. If they do burn, simply start again with fresh spices.

2 green, unripe mangoes, peeled and sliced (2 cups)

4 shallots, thinly sliced (about ½ cup)

4 Indian or Thai green chiles, halved lengthwise

1 (1-inch) piece ginger, peeled and cut into thin matchsticks

3 cloves garlic, cut into thin matchsticks

3 Tbsp coconut vinegar or white vinegar

1½ tsp salt

3 cups coconut milk

1 Tbsp coconut oil

1½ tsp black mustard seeds

4 dried red chiles, snapped in half

20 curry leaves, plus extra for garnish

Fried Onions (page 42), for garnish (optional)

To serve
Basmati Rice (page 156)

SERVES 4–6

Mango Curry
മാങ്ങ കറി

Every house in my Thrissur neighborhood had one or two mango trees. Some were sweet for eating right off the branch, and some were sour, used for pickling and cooking. This vibrantly colored mango curry is authentically Keralan, and one we'd typically pair with a fish curry and accompany with rice. The recipe calls for coconut vinegar, increasingly found in supermarkets and in health food shops, but you may substitute white vinegar if you can't locate a bottle—though do try!

IN A BOWL, combine mangoes, shallots, green chiles, ginger, garlic, vinegar, and salt and mix well. Set aside for 2 hours.

In a large saucepan, combine mango mixture and coconut milk and bring to a boil. Reduce heat and simmer for 5 minutes, or until mangoes are softened.

Have a splash guard and measured spices nearby. Heat oil in a small frying pan over medium-high heat until nearly smoking. Immediately reduce heat to medium. (You can test the heat of the oil by dropping in a couple of seeds. The oil is at the correct temperature when the seeds crackle, but do not burn.) Add mustard seeds and temper for a few seconds, until they stop popping. (Cover with the splash guard, if needed.) Add red chiles and curry leaves and cook for 15–20 seconds. Add the tempered spice mixture to the saucepan and stir to combine.

Garnish with curry leaves and fried onions (if using). Serve with rice.

Tempering is a traditional method of extracting optimal flavor from Indian spices, and it is a skill learned with practice! Reducing the heat a little before adding the spices prevents the spices from burning and adding a bitterness to your dish. If they do burn, simply start again with fresh spices.

SERVES 4

Ooty Mushroom Curry
ഊട്ടി കൂൺ കറി

When I came to Canada, I was astonished by the variety of mushrooms in the markets. We created this delicious mild and creamy curry at Coconut Lagoon, naming it for the area in which Tamil Nadu's largest mushroom farm is found. Feel free to use humble button mushrooms or any other cultivated, seasonal variety.

Gravy Heat oil in a heavy-bottomed frying pan over medium heat, then add cinnamon, cardamom, cloves, and star anise and toast for 1–2 minutes, until fragrant. Add ginger and garlic and sauté for 2 minutes.

Stir in onions and salt and sauté for 10 minutes, until softened and translucent. Stir in coriander, turmeric, chili powder, and mace and cook, stirring well, for 1 minute.

Add tomatoes and cook, stirring, for 2 minutes. Remove from heat and set aside. (The gravy can be stored in an airtight container in the fridge up to 4 days.)

Mushroom curry Have a splash guard and measured spices nearby. Heat oil in a small frying pan over medium-high heat until nearly smoking. Immediately reduce heat to medium. (You can test the heat of the oil by dropping in a couple of seeds. The oil is at the correct temperature when the seeds crackle, but do not burn.) Add mustard and cumin seeds and temper for a few seconds, until they stop popping. (Cover with the splash guard, if needed.) Transfer the spices to a large, heavy-bottomed skillet.

Add curry leaves and mushrooms and sauté over medium heat for 1½ minutes, until mushrooms are softened. Stir in coriander, chili powder, and turmeric and cook for another 2 minutes. Pour in gravy and stir to combine.

Pour in coconut milk and bring to a boil. Remove from heat. Season with fenugreek leaves, salt, and lemon juice.

Garnish with cilantro and serve with rice.

Gravy

5 Tbsp vegetable oil

1 cinnamon stick, broken in half

7 green cardamom pods

9 cloves

½ star anise

1 (1-inch) piece ginger, peeled and finely chopped

8 cloves garlic, finely chopped

3 onions, finely chopped

1 Tbsp salt

2 Tbsp ground coriander

1 Tbsp ground turmeric

1½ tsp red chili powder

Pinch of mace

2 large ripe tomatoes, chopped

Mushroom curry

3 Tbsp coconut oil

1 tsp black mustard seeds

½ tsp cumin seeds

12 curry leaves

1 lb button or cremini mushrooms, quartered (5 cups)

1 Tbsp ground coriander

½ tsp red chili powder

½ tsp ground turmeric

½ cup Gravy (see here)

¾ cup coconut milk

1 tsp dried fenugreek leaves (*kasuri methi*)

½ tsp salt

½ tsp fresh lemon juice

Cilantro, for garnish

To serve

Basmati Rice (page 156)

> **Tempering** is a traditional method of extracting optimal flavor from Indian spices. Reducing the heat a little before adding the spices prevents the spices from burning. If they do burn, simply start again with fresh spices.

2 cups dried red lentils, rinsed

½ cup coconut oil

1 Tbsp cumin seeds

3 cloves garlic, coarsely chopped

1 Tbsp chopped ginger

2 Indian or Thai green chiles, finely chopped

12 curry leaves

2½ onions, finely chopped (1½ cups)

½ tsp salt

½ tsp ground turmeric

1 cup chopped spinach leaves

1 cup coconut milk

½ tsp fresh lemon juice

1 Tbsp Ghee (page 41)

2 Tbsp Fried Onions (page 42), for garnish (optional)

To serve
Basmati Rice (page 156)

SERVES 4

Masoor Dal and Spinach Curry
പരിപ്പ് ചീര കറി

Mild and lightly spiced, the red lentils (*masoor dal*) in this dish cook up in no time at all. Turmeric and fresh spinach lend their lovely colors, but no dal dish is complete without a drizzle of ghee and the lift of lemon. If you wish, top it with fried onions for a sweet, crunchy finish.

IN A LARGE saucepan, combine lentils and 6 cups of lightly salted water and bring to a boil. Reduce heat to medium-low and simmer, uncovered, for 12–15 minutes, until lentils are tender. (If necessary, add more water to keep lentils covered.)

Meanwhile, heat oil in a frying pan over medium heat. Add cumin and toast for 30 seconds. Add garlic, ginger, chiles, and curry leaves and sauté for 1 minute. Stir in onions and salt and cook for 7 minutes, until softened and translucent. Add turmeric and spinach and sauté for 1 minute. Stir in cooked red lentils.

Pour in coconut milk and bring to a boil. Stir in lemon juice and ghee, then remove from heat. Season with salt to taste.

Garnish with fried onions (if using) and serve with rice.

sea
കടൽ

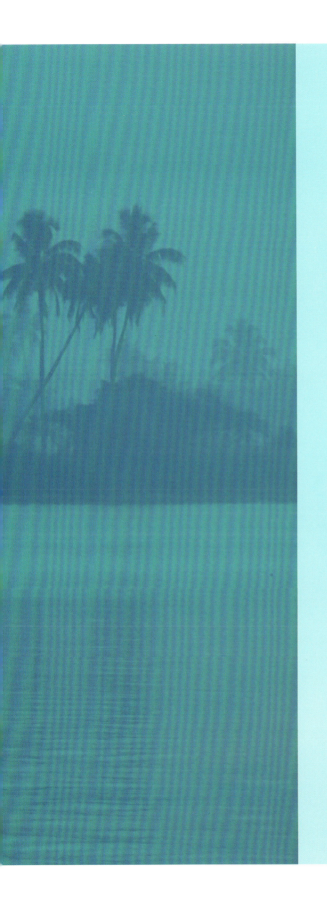

118 **Fish Roasted in Banana Leaf**
121 **Travancore Fish Curry**
122 **Thrissur-Style Salmon Curry**
125 **Coconut Lagoon Mussels**
126 **Shrimp Malabar**
129 **Tamarind Shrimp Masala**
130 **Shrimp Mango Curry**
131 **Lobster Masala**

4 (4–6-oz) tilapia fillets

2 Tbsp coconut oil

2 large shallots, finely chopped

1 Tbsp Ginger-Garlic Paste (page 42)

1–2 Indian or Thai green chiles, halved lengthwise

20 curry leaves

1½ tsp ground turmeric

1½ tsp red chili powder

1 large ripe tomato, finely chopped

1 tsp salt

1½ tsp fresh lime juice

½ cup coconut milk

4 banana leaves, wiped clean with damp towel

To serve
Matta Rice (page 157), Basmati Rice (page 156), or Malabar Parathas (page 60)

Mango Pickle (page 50) or Lemon and Date Pickle (page 51)

SERVES 4

Fish Roasted in Banana Leaf
ഇലയിൽ പൊതിഞ്ഞ മീൻ പൊരിച്ചത്

This is a traditional way of serving fish in Kerala: a piece of fish is wrapped in banana leaf, which acts like parchment paper to seal in the juices and infuse the fish with the flavors of the masala and the leaf. Source fresh or frozen banana leaves at your Asian grocer or in the frozen section of many supermarkets. If you choose a thicker fish or use a whole fish, adjust the cooking time, roughly following the rule of ten minutes per inch of thickness.

CLEAN, WASH, AND pat dry the fish fillets, and set aside.

Heat oil in a frying pan over medium-high heat. Add shallots, ginger-garlic paste, chiles, and curry leaves and sauté for 2 minutes, until shallots are softened. Add turmeric and chili powder and stir well, cooking for 1 more minute. Add tomatoes and salt and cook for 2 minutes. Stir in lime juice and coconut milk, bring to a boil, and cook for 1 minute, until the sauce is thick.

To soften the banana leaves (so they won't tear when folded), warm them by passing each one over a gas flame (being careful not to scorch them). (Alternatively, warm them a few seconds on each side in a large, dry frying pan over medium-high heat, until they turn shiny and pliable.) Once softened, lay the leaves on a clean work surface.

In the center of each leaf, spoon a dollop of the masala. Place the fish on top of the masala, then spoon more masala on top of the fish. Fold the leaf to enclose the fish in a neat, sealed parcel: east and west together, then north and south like a rectangular envelope.

Place parcel, fold side down, in a dry frying pan over medium-high heat and cook for 3 minutes. Carefully flip the parcel and cook for another 3 minutes. Set aside for 5–10 minutes to rest.

To serve, let your guests unwrap the fish themselves and offer a side plate for the discarded leaves. Serve with rice or bread and pickles.

SERVES 4

Travancore Fish Curry
ട്രാവൻകൂർ ഫിഷ് കറി

Red, hot, and fiery! From the Travancore region of southern Kerala, home of my chef de cuisine, Rajesh, this famous fish is seasoned, thickened, and colored with Kashmiri chili powder, made sour with kudampuli (Malabar tamarind), and soothed with rich coconut milk. Traditionally, it's made with kingfish, but we've used wild, line-caught Atlantic cod as a sustainable substitute.

IN A SMALL bowl, combine kudampuli and about ⅓ cup hot water (or just enough to cover) and set aside for 15–20 minutes to soften. If the pieces are large, cut them into 2–3 smaller pieces, then return to the soaking water.

Heat oil in a saucepan over medium heat. Add ginger, garlic, curry leaves, and chiles and sauté for 2 minutes.

In a small bowl, combine chili powders, turmeric, and 1 cup water and mix into a paste. Add the paste to the pan and cook for 1–2 minutes, stirring continuously, until the raw smell is cooked off.

Add 1 cup of water, salt, and the kudampuli pieces, with their soaking water. Increase heat and boil for 4–5 minutes, until slightly thickened. Reduce heat to medium, add cod and simmer for 6–8 minutes, or until cod is just cooked. Pour in coconut milk, increase heat, and bring to a boil. Immediately remove from heat.

Garnish with fresh mint (or cilantro). Serve with rice or bread and pickle.

6–7 kudampuli (Malabar tamarind)

1 Tbsp coconut oil

1 (2-inch) piece ginger, peeled and cut into matchsticks

5 cloves garlic, finely chopped

10 curry leaves

2 Indian or Thai green chiles, halved lengthwise

½ cup Kashmiri chili powder

1 tsp red chili powder

1 tsp ground turmeric

1 Tbsp salt

2 lbs fresh skinless cod, cut into large chunks

1 cup coconut milk

Fresh mint or cilantro leaves, for garnish

To serve
Matta Rice (page 157) or Malabar Parathas (page 60)

Lemon and Date Pickle (page 51)

SERVES 4

4 kudampuli (Malabar tamarind)

3 Tbsp coconut oil

2 (2-inch) pieces ginger, peeled and cut into matchsticks

4–6 cloves garlic, cut into matchsticks

2 Indian or Thai green chiles, chopped

15 curry leaves, coarsely chopped, plus extra for garnish

1½ tsp red chili powder

1 tsp ground turmeric

1 tsp salt, plus extra to taste

1 lb skinless salmon fillets, cut into 1-inch cubes

½ cup coconut milk

1 tomato, quartered, seeded, and thinly sliced lengthwise, for garnish (optional)

To serve
Basmati Rice (page 156)

Thrissur-Style Salmon Curry
തൃശൂർ -സ്റ്റൈൽ സാൽമൺ കറി

I first tasted salmon in Saudi Arabia, where it was occasionally flown in to the kitchens of the Oasis Resorts. And, of course, when I came to Canada, I learned how prized and important this great fish was, in many Canadian communities, and how beautifully it behaved in a curry. Added at the end, the chunks of salmon cook in the hot and sour sauce, stay moist and soft, and hold their shape well. Prepared with Atlantic or wild Pacific salmon, this Thrissur-style fish curry is a Coconut Lagoon fan favorite.

IN A SMALL bowl, combine kudampuli and ¼ cup hot water (or just enough to cover) and set aside for 15–20 minutes to soften. If the pieces are large, cut them into 2–3 smaller pieces, then return to soaking water.

Heat oil in a heavy-bottomed frying pan over medium heat. Add ginger, garlic, chiles, and curry leaves and sauté for 2–3 minutes, until the leaves are wilted and flavors are released.

Add chili powder and turmeric and stir for another 30 seconds, until the raw smell is cooked off. Pour in 1½ cups water, the kudampuli pieces, with their soaking water, and salt and bring to a boil. Reduce heat and simmer for 3 minutes.

Add salmon and simmer for 4–5 minutes, or until fish is just cooked. Pour in coconut milk, bring back to a boil, and immediately remove from heat. Season with salt to taste.

Garnish with curry leaves and tomato strips (if using) and serve with rice.

SERVES 4

Coconut Lagoon Mussels
കോകനട്ട് ലഗൂൺ മസ്സൽസ്

We created this dish to give our mussels from Canada's East Coast some Kerala flavors. They are steamed in a spiced and smoky Clamato broth and finished with rich, thick coconut cream. Serve with steamed rice or, better yet, use parathas to soak up the broth.

IN A SMALL bowl, combine kudampuli and ¼ cup hot water (or just enough to cover) and set aside for 15–20 minutes to soften. If the pieces are large, cut them into 2–3 smaller pieces, then return to soaking water. Set aside.

Heat oil in a wok or frying pan over medium heat. Add ginger, garlic, chiles, and curry leaves and sauté for 2–3 minutes, until the leaves are wilted and flavors are released.

Add onions and sauté for 2 minutes. Stir in chili powder, cooking for another 30 seconds, until the raw smell is cooked off.

Pour in Clamato juice, increase heat to high, and bring to a boil. Stir in kudampuli pieces, with their soaking water, and the mussels. Cover and cook for 4 minutes, until mussels have just opened. Pour in coconut cream and cook uncovered for 1 more minute. Discard any unopened mussels. Season with salt to taste.

Garnish with curry leaves and serve immediately with rice or bread.

2 kudampuli (Malabar tamarind)

2 Tbsp coconut oil

1 (1-inch) piece ginger, peeled and cut into matchsticks

6 cloves garlic, cut into matchsticks

2 Indian or Thai green chiles, coarsely chopped

10 curry leaves, plus extra for garnish

1 onion, finely sliced

½ tsp red chili powder

1 cup Clamato juice

1 lb live mussels, scrubbed clean and rinsed well

¼ cup coconut cream

Salt, to taste

To serve
Basmati Rice (page 156), Matta Rice (page 157), or Malabar Parathas (page 60)

SERVES 4

4 kudampuli (Malabar tamarind)

½ cup fresh or frozen grated coconut

¼ cup finely chopped shallots

1 tsp ground turmeric

1 tsp red chili powder

½ tsp salt

1 Tbsp coconut oil

3 cloves garlic, finely chopped

1½ tsp finely chopped ginger

8 curry leaves, plus extra for garnish

1 lb medium shrimp, shelled and deveined, with tails intact

½ large ripe tomato, finely chopped, for garnish

Shrimp Malabar

മലബാർ ചെമ്മീൻ കറി

The entire coastline of Kerala was once known by the name "Malabar." Today, the region stretches from Palakkad in the south to Kasaragod in the north, flanked by the Arabian Sea and the Western Ghats. Seafood and coconut and spices are at the heart of Malabar cuisine and this recipe unites them, along with kudampuli, or Malabar tamarind, which is so ubiquitous in Kerala fish cooking.

My mother would sun-dry the small, pumpkin-shaped tamarinds, freshly plucked and seeded when ripe, from our garden trees in May, and, when the rains of the Southwest Monsoon would begin, she'd smoke the sun-shriveled fruit under our chimney for weeks. (It keeps indefinitely.) Here, it lends its distinctively sour kick to the dish.

IN A SMALL bowl, combine kudampuli and ¼ cup hot water (or just enough to cover) and set aside for 15–20 minutes to soften. If the pieces are large, cut them into 2–3 smaller pieces, then return to soaking water.

In a food processor, combine coconut, shallots, turmeric, chili powder, and salt and purée into a smooth paste. Set aside.

Heat oil in a frying pan over medium heat. Add garlic, ginger, and curry leaves and sauté for 1 minute. Add coconut-chili paste and sauté for 2 minutes. Add shrimp and kudampuli pieces, with their soaking water, and simmer for 3 minutes.

Garnish with curry leaves and tomatoes and serve.

SERVES 4

Tamarind Shrimp Masala

റ്റമറൈൻഡ് ചെമ്മീൻ മസാല

My most vivid memory of my grandmother is of her peeling, peeling, endlessly peeling the tiny prawns we bought at the markets in Thrissur. At Coconut Lagoon, we use meaty Ocean Wise–certified black tiger shrimp. The foundation of any good curry or masala begins with its aromatics and spices, but this hearty tomato-based curry is made exceptional with sour tamarind, which also acts as a preservative.

Tamarind paste Place tamarind in a small bowl, add enough boiling water to cover, and set aside for 20–30 minutes to soften. Transfer softened pulp to a fine-mesh strainer set over a clean bowl. Using a spoon or spatula, push the pulp through the strainer to separate the tamarind paste from its fibers (and occasional seeds). Scrape the paste from the underside of the strainer to collect as much as you can. Discard the fibers and set the paste aside.

Shrimp masala In a bowl, combine shrimp, ½ tsp salt, ½ tsp chili powder, and ½ tsp turmeric and mix gently to coat the shrimp. Set aside to marinate for 20 minutes.

Heat ⅓ cup oil in a frying pan over medium-high heat. Add shrimp and stir-fry for 1 minute, until pink. Transfer to a plate and set aside.

Have a splash guard and measured spices nearby. Heat remaining ⅓ cup oil in a saucepan over medium-high heat until nearly smoking. Immediately reduce heat to medium. (You can test the heat of the oil by dropping in a couple of seeds. The oil is at the correct temperature when the seeds crackle, but do not burn.) Add mustard seeds and temper for a few seconds, until they stop popping. (Cover with the splash guard, if needed.) Add fenugreek seeds and temper another 30 seconds. Add onions, garlic, ginger, curry leaves, and tomatoes and sauté for 2 minutes.

Add the remaining 3½ tsp chili powder, ½ tsp turmeric, and the coriander and stir for 1 minute. Add tamarind paste. Season with the remaining 2½ tsp salt and bring to a boil. Add shrimp, reduce heat to medium, and simmer for 1 minute.

Adjust seasoning if needed, garnish with cilantro, and serve immediately with rice.

Tamarind paste

8 oz tamarind pulp, broken into small chunks

Shrimp masala

1 lb medium shrimp, shelled and deveined, with tails intact

3 tsp salt, plus extra to taste (divided)

4 tsp red chili powder (divided)

1 tsp ground turmeric (divided)

⅔ cup coconut oil (divided)

½ tsp black mustard seeds

½ tsp fenugreek seeds

1 onion, thinly sliced

1 clove garlic, coarsely chopped

1 (½-inch) piece ginger, peeled and coarsely chopped

15 curry leaves

1 large ripe tomato, chopped

1 tsp ground coriander

¼ cup Tamarind Paste (see here)

Chopped cilantro leaves, for garnish

To serve

Basmati Rice (page 156)

> **Tempering** is a traditional method of extracting optimal flavor from Indian spices, and it is a skill learned with practice! Reducing the heat a little before adding the spices prevents the spices from burning and adding a bitterness to your dish. If they do burn, simply start again with fresh spices.

SERVES 4

1 lb medium shrimp, shelled and deveined

1½ tsp fresh lime juice

1 Tbsp coconut oil

1½ tsp black mustard seeds

Pinch of fenugreek seeds

1 onion, finely chopped (½ cup)

3 cloves garlic, coarsely chopped

1 (1-inch) piece ginger, peeled and coarsely chopped

20 curry leaves

1 tsp ground turmeric

1 tsp ground coriander

½ tsp red chili powder

½ cup sliced green, unripe mangoes

½ cup coconut milk

1 tsp salt, plus extra to taste

To serve
Matta Rice (page 157)
Malabar Parathas (page 60)

Shrimp Mango Curry

ചെമ്മീൻ മാങ്ങ കറി

Also known as chemmeen mango curry, this classic recipe is a summer staple when mangoes are optimally sweet and in abundance. The green mango lends its sour notes to the shrimp, while the coconut milk balances that sour with a sweet creaminess. Best of all, this tasty recipe delivers all the complexities of a curry in a fraction of the time.

IN A SMALL bowl, combine shrimp and lime juice. Cover and marinate in the fridge for 1 hour.

Have a splash guard and measured spices nearby. Heat oil in a small frying pan over medium-high heat until nearly smoking. Immediately reduce heat to medium. (You can test the heat of the oil by dropping in a couple of seeds. The oil is at the correct temperature when the seeds crackle, but do not burn.) Add mustard seeds and temper for a few seconds, until they stop popping. (Cover with the splash guard, if needed.) Add fenugreek seeds and temper another 30 seconds. Add onions, garlic, ginger, and curry leaves and sauté for 2 minutes, until fragrant. Add turmeric, coriander, and chili powder and stir for 1 minute, until the raw smell is cooked off. Transfer to a large heavy-bottomed skillet.

Increase heat to high. Add shrimp and mango slices and sauté for 1 minute. Pour in coconut milk, bring to a boil, and cook for 1 minute, or until shrimp turns pink. Add salt and adjust seasoning to taste.

Serve with rice and parathas.

> **Tempering** is a traditional method of extracting optimal flavor from Indian spices, and it is a skill learned with practice! Reducing the heat a little before adding the spices prevents the spices from burning and adding a bitterness to your dish. If they do burn, simply start again with fresh spices.

SERVES 2

Lobster Masala

ലോബ്സ്റ്റർ മസാല

In Kerala, all the best lobster was exported. What we could get, when I was a child, was sourced directly from the fishermen at the small docks that traced the shoreline, or in the fish markets in our coastal areas—and it was expensive. This dish would have been reserved for a special occasion in my family.

Velvety smooth, with slivers of fresh ginger and crinkly fried curry leaves for texture and fragrance, this wonderfully rich dish is perfect for a decadent dinner. We use lobster tail meat here and at the restaurant, but you could substitute crabmeat or shrimp.

IN A SMALL bowl, combine kudampuli and ¼ cup hot water (or just enough to cover) and set aside for 15–20 minutes to soften. If the pieces are large, cut them into 2–3 smaller pieces, then return to soaking water. Set aside.

Heat oil in a large frying pan over medium heat. Add ginger, garlic, chiles, and curry leaves and sauté for 1 minute. Add onions and salt and cook for 2 minutes, until the raw smell is cooked off. Stir in tomatoes and cook for 3 minutes.

Add coriander, chili powder, and turmeric and cook for another 2 minutes. Add lobster and the kudampuli pieces, with their soaking water. Simmer for 5 minutes, covered, until lobster is tender. Stir in coconut milk, bring to a boil, and remove from heat.

Garnish with cilantro and serve with rice.

2 kudampuli (Malabar tamarind)

1 Tbsp coconut oil

1 tsp finely chopped ginger

1 clove garlic, finely chopped

2 Indian or Thai green chiles, halved lengthwise

8 curry leaves

1 onion, finely chopped

1 tsp salt

1 large ripe tomato, finely chopped

2 tsp ground coriander

1 tsp Kashmiri chili powder

½ tsp ground turmeric

½ lb lobster tail meat (cut in chunks)

½ cup coconut milk

Cilantro leaves, for garnish

To serve
Lemon Rice (page 160) or Matta Rice (page 157)

land
ഭൂമി

- 134 Chicken Chettinad
- 135 Cook's Curry
- 136 Nadan Kozhi Curry
- 139 Coconut Lagoon Butter Chicken
- 140 Nilgiri Chicken
- 143 Duck Kumarakom
- 144 Kerala Beef Fry
- 146 Beef Curry
- 149 Lamb with Fennel Seeds
- 151 Malabar Pepper Lamb
- 152 Lamb Korma

SERVES 4

Chettinad masala
¼ cup raw cashew nuts
8 dried red chiles, snapped in half
1 (1-inch) cinnamon stick
¼ cup coriander seeds
3 Tbsp black peppercorns
4 tsp cloves
4 tsp cumin seeds
4 tsp fennel seeds
2 tsp ground turmeric
Salt, to taste

Chicken
2 Tbsp coconut oil
2 large onions, thinly sliced (2 cups)
2 Tbsp Ginger-Garlic Paste (page 42)
20 curry leaves
1 large ripe tomato, coarsely chopped
Pinch of ground turmeric
1 lb boneless, skinless chicken breast, cubed
1 Tbsp fresh lemon juice
Chettinad Masala (see here)
Coarsely chopped cilantro, for garnish

To serve
Basmati Rice (page 156)

Chicken Chettinad

ചിക്കൻ ചെട്ടിനാട്

From the Chettinad region of Tamil Nadu, this fiery curry is the go-to dish on cold nights. The secret weapon is the dry-roasting of the spices before you pulse them into a paste, and the lift of lemon juice at the end is a welcome finish.

Chettinad masala In a frying pan, combine all ingredients and dry-roast over medium heat for 2–3 minutes. Set aside to cool. Transfer to a food processor, add 2 Tbsp water, and process until a thick, coarse paste forms. Set aside.

Chicken Heat oil in a frying pan over medium-high heat. Add onions and sauté for 2 minutes, until browned. Reduce heat to medium. Add ginger-garlic paste and curry leaves and sauté for 1–2 minutes until fragrant and the masala paste has turned light brown.

Add tomatoes and turmeric and cook for 2–3 minutes more. Add chicken, stir well, and cook for 8 minutes, until chicken is par-cooked. Stir in the masala paste and simmer, stirring occasionally, for another 10 minutes, or until the chicken is cooked through. Stir in lemon juice.

Garnish with cilantro leaves. Serve with rice.

SERVES 4–6

Cook's Curry
കുക്ക്സ് കറി

I prepared this curry for a staff meal one night, using the dark meat from leftover chicken, and it's been a hit ever since. Fast, filling, and flavorful, this stew is designed for fueling up ahead of service (or ahead of soccer practice). Made in one pot, its marinade is versatile enough to suit a number of applications, and you could easily substitute leftover uncooked lamb or beef, or even root vegetables for a vegetarian feast.

Marinade In a bowl, combine all ingredients and mix well.

Chicken Put chicken into a large bowl, rub marinade over the pieces, and set aside for 20–30 minutes.

Transfer chicken to a stockpot and add salt and enough cold water to cover by 1 inch. Bring to a boil, reduce heat, and simmer for 30 minutes, or until chicken is cooked and sauce is reduced by a half. (Cooking time will vary depending on the size of the chicken pieces. Test the thighs by poking with a knife: if the meat is still pink, cook a little longer.)

Garnish with cilantro and serve the chicken and sauce with rice.

Marinade

8 cloves garlic, coarsely chopped

4 Indian or Thai green chiles, halved lengthwise

2 onions, thinly sliced

2 tomatoes, chopped

20 curry leaves

1 Tbsp finely chopped ginger

3 Tbsp ground coriander

1 Tbsp ground turmeric

1½ tsp red chili powder

1½ tsp coarsely ground black pepper

1½ tsp Garam Masala (page 41)

2 Tbsp white vinegar

1 Tbsp vegetable oil

Chicken

1 (2-lb) whole chicken, skin removed and cut into 8–10 pieces

Marinade (see here)

2 tsp salt

Chopped cilantro, for garnish

To serve

Basmati Rice (page 156)

½ cup coconut oil

10 green cardamom pods

6 whole cloves

1 (2-inch) cinnamon stick

1 star anise

3 Tbsp chopped ginger

8 cloves garlic, coarsely chopped

3 Indian or Thai green chiles, halved lengthwise

4 onions, coarsely chopped (2½ cups)

20 curry leaves, plus extra for garnish

1 tsp salt, plus extra to taste

¼ cup ground coriander

1 Tbsp red chili powder

1½ tsp ground turmeric

1 large ripe tomato, chopped

1 (2-lb) whole chicken, cut into 8–10 pieces, or 2 lbs bone-in chicken thighs, skin removed

1 cup coconut milk

1½ tsp coarsely ground black pepper

1½ tsp Garam Masala (page 41)

1½ tsp fresh lemon juice

To serve
Malabar Parathas (page 60), Chapatis (page 55), or Pooris (page 59)

SERVES 4–6

Nadan Kozhi Curry

നാടൻ കോഴി കറി

Nadan means "homestyle," and this curry has been served in Kerala homes for centuries. All of our most prized ingredients—curry leaves, cardamom, peppercorns, coconut milk—come together in one beautifully flavorful, thick, and rustic dish. You could use chicken breasts, if you prefer, but the flavor is so much better with bone-in chicken. Use a whole chicken, cut into sections, or bone-in thighs. If time allows, let the curry rest overnight to develop the flavors and serve with bread to sop up the sauce.

HEAT OIL IN a wok or heavy-bottomed frying pan over medium heat. Add cardamom, cloves, cinnamon, and star anise and cook, stirring, for 1 minute, or until fragrant. Add ginger, garlic, and chiles and sauté for 1 more minute.

Add onions, curry leaves, and salt and sauté for 7 minutes, until onions are softened and translucent. Add coriander, chili powder, and turmeric and cook for 1–2 minutes, until the raw smell is cooked off. Stir in tomatoes and chicken and pour in 1 cup water. Bring to a boil, then reduce heat and cover. Simmer for 20 minutes, or until chicken is cooked through. (Cooking time will vary, depending on chicken used and size of pieces.)

Pour in coconut milk and bring back to a boil. Remove from heat and stir in pepper, garam masala, and lemon juice. Season with salt to taste.

Garnish with curry leaves and serve with parathas, chapatis, or pooris.

SERVES 4–6

Coconut Lagoon Butter Chicken

കോകനട്ട് ലഗൂൺ ബട്ടർ ചിക്കൻ

We would have been much better off, financially, if we'd had butter chicken on the menu from the very beginning. After four years of patiently explaining to our guests that butter chicken was a north Indian dish and that we were a south Indian restaurant, we finally created our own version. The truth is, this gentle dish introduces children to the flavors of India, serving as a stepping stone for them (and their parents!) to then dig a little deeper into the menu. And besides, my son Mathew, raised on Kerala cuisine, claims butter chicken is his hands-down favorite. So this is for him.

IN A SAUCEPAN, combine cashews and 4 cups water and bring to a boil over high heat. Reduce heat and simmer for 5 minutes, until nuts have softened. Strain and set aside to cool. Transfer to a food processor or blender and purée until smooth.

In a large bowl, combine chicken, yogurt, chili powder, turmeric, salt, and oil and mix well until chicken pieces are fully coated. Cover and refrigerate for at least 6 hours.

Preheat oven to 350°F. Line a baking sheet with parchment paper.

Place chicken on prepared baking sheet and bake for 15 minutes, until par-cooked.

Melt butter in a saucepan over medium-high heat. Add onions and sauté for 3 minutes. Reduce heat to medium. Add ginger-garlic paste and cook for another 3 minutes. Stir in coriander, cooking for 1 more minute.

Add tomatoes and tomato paste and cook for 5 minutes. Stir in 2 Tbsp cashew paste, sugar, fenugreek leaves, cumin, and chaat masala and cook for 1 minute. (Leftover cashew paste can be stored in an airtight container in the fridge for up to 5 days.) Add chicken and milk and bring to a boil. Reduce heat and simmer for 8 minutes, or until chicken is cooked through but still juicy and tender. Season with salt to taste.

Garnish with cilantro and serve with rice.

---

2 cups raw cashew nuts

2 lbs boneless, skinless chicken breasts, cut into 1-inch cubes

3 Tbsp plain yogurt

½ tsp red chili powder

½ tsp ground turmeric

½ tsp salt, plus extra to taste

1 tsp coconut oil

¼ cup (½ stick) unsalted butter

2 small onions, chopped

1½ tsp Ginger-Garlic Paste (page 42)

1½ tsp ground coriander

2 tomatoes, finely chopped

3 Tbsp tomato paste

1½ tsp sugar

1½ tsp dried fenugreek leaves (*kasuri methi*)

½ tsp ground cumin

½ tsp chaat masala

3 cups milk

Chopped cilantro, for garnish

To serve
Basmati Rice (page 156)

½ cup coconut oil

10 green cardamom pods

6 cloves

1 (1-inch) cinnamon stick

1 star anise

6 Tbsp Ginger-Garlic Paste (page 42)

6–10 Indian or Thai green chiles, finely chopped

4 onions, finely chopped

1 Tbsp salt

¼ cup ground coriander

1½ tsp ground turmeric

¾ cup plain yogurt

1 cup chopped cilantro, plus extra for garnish

¼ cup chopped mint, plus extra for garnish

2 lbs boneless, skinless chicken breasts, or combination of breasts and leg meat, cubed

1 cup coconut cream

1½ tsp fresh lemon juice

1½ tsp coarsely ground black pepper

1½ tsp ground cumin

To serve
Basmati Rice (page 156) or Lemon Rice (page 160)

SERVES 4–6

Nilgiri Chicken
നീലഗിരി ചിക്കൻ

Nilgiri, which means "blue mountains," is the name given to the range that separates the states of Tamil Nadu, Karnataka, and Kerala. This dish comes from that cooler, hilly country, beneath the higher tea plantations, where leafy greens grow well in the misty air. The recipe, from my long-time chef de cuisine, Rajesh, combines chicken with cilantro, mint, green chiles, and yogurt and is brightened with lemon. Fresh-tasting and aromatic, it's an ideal dish in the summer when fresh herbs are abundant.

HEAT OIL IN a heavy-bottomed frying pan over medium heat. Add cardamom, cloves, cinnamon, and star anise and roast for 1 minute, until fragrant. Add ginger-garlic paste and chiles and sauté for 1–2 minutes. Add onions and salt and cook for 7 minutes, stirring, until onions are softened and translucent.

Add coriander and turmeric and stir well to prevent them from burning or sticking to the bottom of the pan. Stir in yogurt, herbs, and chicken and mix well.

Pour in ½ cup water and simmer, covered, for 15 minutes over medium heat, until chicken is cooked. Pour in coconut cream and bring back to a boil. Add lemon juice, pepper, and cumin.

Serve with rice.

SERVES 4–6

Duck Kumarakom
ഡക്ക് കുമരകം

The palm-fringed backwaters of Kumarakom and Alappuzha are a picturesque labyrinth of lagoons, rivers, lakes, and canals that run parallel to the Arabian Sea. Herds of ducks in these waters are often "shepherded" to their feeding grounds by men in canoes.

Duck is a luxury in Kerala, and a dish my family would serve for special occasions only: no wedding is a wedding without duck! This recipe—from my mother-in-law, who grew up in the Alappuzha region—uses the whole bird, slowly simmered with lots of onions and pepper in a thick coconut curry sauce.

HEAT OIL IN a heavy-bottomed frying pan over medium heat. Add the cardamom, cinnamon, and fennel seeds and roast for 1 minute, until fragrant. Add onions, ginger, and chiles and sauté for 2 minutes.

Add coriander, black pepper, turmeric, and chili powder and roast, stirring well, for 1 minute, until fragrant. Stir in tomatoes and cook for 1 more minute.

Add duck, coconut milk, and salt and stir well. Reduce heat to medium-low, cover and simmer gently for 25 minutes, or until duck is cooked. Finish with lemon juice and garam masala.

Serve with parathas or chapatis and wash it down with a good local beer!

3 Tbsp coconut oil

12 green cardamom pods

1 (2-inch) cinnamon stick

1 tsp fennel seeds

3 large onions, thinly sliced

2 Tbsp finely chopped ginger

3–4 Indian or Thai green chiles, halved lengthwise

2 Tbsp ground coriander

2 tsp coarsely ground black pepper

½ tsp ground turmeric

½ tsp red chili powder

2 large tomatoes, chopped

2 lbs boneless, skinless duck breasts, cut into 1-inch cubes

1½ cups coconut milk

1 Tbsp salt

1 Tbsp fresh lemon juice

½ tsp Garam Masala (page 41)

To serve
Malabar Parathas (page 60) or Chapatis (page 55)

SERVES 6

½ cup fresh or frozen coconut chunks

¼ cup ground coriander

1 Tbsp red chili powder

1½ tsp ground turmeric

2 lbs beef tenderloin tips, cut into 1-inch cubes

1½ tsp salt

1½ cups coconut oil

2 dried red chiles, snapped in half

20 curry leaves

½ tsp fennel seeds

2 large onions, coarsely chopped

3 cloves garlic, coarsely chopped

1 Tbsp finely chopped ginger

1 Tbsp fresh lemon juice

1 Tbsp coarsely ground black pepper

1 tsp Garam Masala (page 41)

Thinly sliced red onions, for garnish

To serve
Chapatis (page 55) or Malabar Parathas (page 60)

Kerala Beef Fry

കേരള ബീഫ് ഫ്രൈ

Despite 55 percent of the population of Kerala identifying as Hindu, beef is widely consumed, and this dish is particularly popular throughout the state. The classic beef fry, also known as *beef ularthiyathu*, is dry, rich, and fiery, and accented with slivers of fresh coconut. I recommend succulent tenderloin tips, but you can also use stewing beef.

USING A VEGETABLE peeler, cut the coconut chunks into thin slivers. Set aside.

In a small bowl, combine coriander, chili powder, and turmeric and mix well.

In a large saucepan, combine beef, half the spice mixture, and salt. Pour in 2 cups water and bring to a boil over high heat. Reduce heat and simmer for 5 minutes until beef is tender. Drain, then set aside.

Heat oil in a large frying pan over medium heat. Add chiles, curry leaves, coconut slivers, and fennel seeds and cook for 30 seconds. Add onions, garlic, and ginger and sauté for 7 minutes, until onions are softened and translucent.

Stir in the remaining half of the spice mixture and cook for 1–2 minutes. Add beef, mix well, and cook over low heat for 4–5 minutes. Remove from the heat, then finish with lemon juice, pepper, and garam masala.

Garnish with red onion and serve with chapatis or parathas.

¼ cup coconut oil

6 onions, coarsely chopped (4 cups)

1½ tsp salt (divided)

¼ cup Ginger-Garlic Paste (page 42)

3–4 Indian or Thai green chiles, coarsely chopped

20 curry leaves, plus extra for garnish

1 Tbsp ground turmeric

1 Tbsp red chili powder

¼ cup ground coriander

½ tsp coarsely ground black pepper

2 large ripe tomatoes, chopped

2 lbs stewing beef or beef tenderloin tips, cut into ½-inch cubes

1 cup coconut milk

1 tsp Garam Masala (page 41)

To serve
Chapatis (page 55) or Malabar Parathas (page 60)

SERVES 4–6

Beef Curry
ബീഫ് കറി

Back home, my mother would stretch out this fragrant stew with lots of potatoes or plantains, to feed our large family on a limited budget. For a Sunday night supper, eaten with chapatis or parathas, it was a favorite of mine. At Coconut Lagoon, we use tenderloin tips for this dish, but stewing beef in a pressure cooker works very well.

HEAT OIL IN a heavy-bottomed frying pan over medium heat. Add onions and ½ tsp salt and sauté for 7 minutes, until softened and translucent. Add ginger-garlic paste, chiles, and curry leaves and cook for another 3 minutes.

Stir in turmeric, chili powder, coriander, and pepper and sauté for 2 minutes. Increase heat to high. Add tomatoes, mix well, and cook for 2 minutes. Add beef and the remaining 1 tsp salt and stir for 3 minutes, until beef is well coated. Pour in 1½ cups water and bring to a boil, then reduce heat to medium-low. Cover and simmer for 30 minutes, or until beef is tender.

Pour in coconut milk and bring to a boil. Reduce heat and simmer 2–3 minutes. Remove from the heat.

Sprinkle garam masala and scatter curry leaves on top and serve with chapatis or parathas.

SERVES 4

Lamb with Fennel Seeds
ലാമ്പ് വിത് ഫെന്നേൽ സീഡ്സ്

Coming from households that can't afford to waste food, we create many of our recipes to deal with leftovers. This flavor-packed stir-fry is a classic example of that: it gives new life and kick to yesterday's roast lamb, tossing the cooked meat with fragrant spices, notably the licorice scent of fennel. The trick is to start with tender chunks of lamb. Here, we've provided a recipe for fresh lamb, but if you are using leftover cooked lamb, you can simply skip straight to sautéing. Serve this dry dish with something saucy, like a dal curry (page 114). And because lamb loves lemon, add a bowl of Lemon Rice (page 160).

IN A LARGE saucepan, combine lamb, coriander, chili powder, 1 tsp salt, pepper, and turmeric. Add 4 cups water and bring to a boil. Reduce heat to medium-low, cover, and simmer for 30–35 minutes. Drain lamb and reserve the cooking liquid.

Heat oil in the same saucepan over medium-high heat. Add garlic, ginger, onions, bell peppers, chiles, curry leaves, fennel seeds, and remaining ½ tsp of salt and sauté for 1–2 minutes, until fragrant. Add lamb and ½ cup of cooking liquid (or water), increase heat, and sauté for 5 minutes, stirring well, until all the liquid has evaporated.

Finish with ground fennel and 'emon juice. Serve with lemon rice.

1 lb boneless leg of lamb or lamb shoulder, cut into cubes

1 Tbsp ground coriander

1½ tsp red chili powder

1½ tsp salt (divided)

½ tsp coarsely ground black pepper

¼ tsp ground turmeric

2 Tbsp vegetable oil

3 cloves garlic, chopped

1 Tbsp chopped ginger

1 onion, cut into thick slices

1 green bell pepper, seeded, deveined, and cut lengthwise into wedges

2 Thai red or orange chiles, halved lengthwise

12 curry leaves

1½ Tbsp fennel seeds

1 Tbsp ground fennel

1 tsp fresh lemon juice

To serve
Lemon Rice (page 160)

SERVES 6–8

Malabar Pepper Lamb
മലബാർ പേപ്പർ ലാമ്പ്

Our famous black pepper is as much the star of this dish as the lamb! Make a stack of Malabar Parathas (page 60) or Chapatis (page 55) to soak up every bit of the sauce. And because cumin is wonderful with pepper, steam some Jeera Rice (page 158) to go alongside.

IN A SMALL bowl, combine coriander, pepper, turmeric, chili powder, and salt. Set aside.

In a stockpot, combine lamb and half the spice mixture and mix well. Pour in water to cover the meat by 1 inch and bring to a boil over high heat. Reduce heat to medium-low and simmer, covered, for 30 minutes, or until lamb is very tender. Drain lamb and reserve the cooking liquid. Set aside.

Heat oil in a large saucepan over medium heat. Add ginger-garlic paste and sauté for 1 minute. Add onions and curry leaves and cook for 2–3 minutes, until onions are lightly brown. Add the remaining spice mixture and stir for 2 minutes, until the raw smell is cooked off.

Stir in tomatoes and cook for 12 minutes. Add the lamb and half the reserved cooking liquid and simmer for another 15 minutes, adding more liquid if necessary to make a nice, thick stew. Remove from the heat.

Stir in lemon juice, garam masala, and sugar and set aside for 10–15 minutes. Season with salt to taste.

Garnish with cilantro and serve with parathas or chapatis and jeera rice.

¾ cup ground coriander

3 Tbsp coarsely ground black pepper

2 Tbsp ground turmeric

4 tsp red chili powder

1 Tbsp salt, plus extra to taste

2 lbs boneless leg of lamb, cut into ½-inch cubes

¼ cup vegetable oil

⅓ cup Ginger-Garlic Paste (page 42)

7–8 onions, coarsely chopped (5 cups)

30 curry leaves (3 sprigs)

3–4 large ripe tomatoes, chopped (3 cups)

3 Tbsp fresh lemon juice

1 Tbsp Garam Masala (page 41)

Pinch of sugar

½ cup chopped cilantro

To serve
Malabar Parathas (page 60) or Chapatis (page 55)
Jeera Rice (page 158)

SERVES 4

Coconut paste
1 cup fresh or frozen grated coconut

1½ tsp Garam Masala (page 41)

1½ tsp ground cumin

¼ tsp ground turmeric

Lamb
2 Tbsp coconut oil

1 Tbsp chopped ginger

1 clove garlic, chopped

4 Indian or Thai green chiles, halved lengthwise

2 small onions, finely chopped (1¼ cups)

2 Tbsp ground coriander

½ tsp ground turmeric

1 lb stewing lamb or leg of lamb, cubed

½ tsp salt

1 cup Coconut Paste (see here)

½ cup coconut milk

Fried Onions (page 42), for garnish

To serve
Basmati Rice (page 156)

Lamb Korma
ലാമ്പ് കുറുമ

Anytime lamb is used in our family, the dish becomes festive! Lamb korma—a signature dish of northern India—is a lovely, mild curry that is often thickened with poppy seeds and rich with cream. We do things a little bit differently at the restaurant. Here, we use both fresh coconut and coconut milk for body and creaminess. Green chiles, rather than red chili powder, give the dish a little heat without altering the delicate color.

Coconut paste In a small bowl, combine the ingredients and blend into a paste. Set aside.

Lamb Heat oil in a frying pan over medium heat. Add ginger, garlic, chiles, and onions and sauté for 2 minutes.

Add coriander and turmeric and cook for 30 seconds. Add lamb and salt, add 3 cups water, and cover. Simmer for 30 minutes on medium-low heat, until lamb is cooked. Stir in coconut paste and cook for 2 minutes. Add coconut milk and bring to a boil. Reduce heat and simmer for 3–4 minutes.

Garnish with fried onions and serve with rice.

rice
നെല്ല്

156 Basmati Rice
157 Matta Rice
158 Jeera Rice
159 Tomato Rice
160 Lemon Rice
161 Curd Rice
162 Lamb Biryani

2 cups basmati rice

1 tsp salt

1½ tsp fresh lemon juice

1½ tsp vegetable oil

SERVES 6

Basmati Rice

ബസ്മതി റൈസ്

The Hindi word for "fragrant" is *bāsmatī*—and with good reason when you consider India's most famous rice. Nutty and intensely aromatic, basmati is the essential rice of north India. Look for extra-long, high-quality, aged basmati, packaged in cloth. The color of the rice should be white, not gray, with a slightly golden hue. There are many methods for cooking basmati. This is mine.

RINSE RICE WELL, at least 3–4 times, until the water runs clear. Put rice, salt, lemon juice, and oil in a large saucepan, add 4 cups water, and bring to a boil, stirring to prevent rice from sticking.

Reduce heat to medium-low and simmer, covered, for 12–15 minutes until rice is cooked. Remove from heat and set aside, covered, for another 8–10 minutes. Remove lid and fluff the grains with a fork. Serve immediately.

SERVES 6

2 cups Matta rice
1½ tsp salt

Matta Rice

മട്ട റൈസ്

Our native matta rice (or Kerala red rice) is grown in the black soils of the Palakkad region of Kerala. The grains are chubby and coarse with a pinkish shell. Highly nutritious and rich in fiber, they require a longer cooking time than basmati. It was my job as a little boy to wash and soak the matta, so it would be ready for cooking when my mother got home. The rice can be found at Indian or Asian food shops.

RINSE RICE WELL, at least 3–4 times, until the water runs clear. Put rice and salt in a large saucepan, add 10 cups water, and bring to a boil, stirring to prevent rice from sticking. Reduce heat to medium-low and simmer, covered, for 50 minutes, stirring occasionally, until cooked through. Drain water, then transfer rice to a serving plate. Serve warm.

1 Tbsp Ghee (page 41)

1½ tsp cumin seeds

10 curry leaves

1 Tbsp Fried Onions (page 42)

3 cups cooked basmati rice

Salt, to taste

Chopped cilantro, for garnish

SERVES 4

Jeera Rice

ജീര റൈസ്

Jeera rice is simply basmati rice flavored with roasted cumin seeds (and curry leaves when made in the south), threaded with fried onions, and garnished with cilantro.

HEAT GHEE IN a wok or frying pan over medium-high heat. Immediately reduce heat to medium. (You can test the heat of the ghee by dropping in a couple of seeds. It is at the correct temperature when the seeds crackle, but do not burn.) Add cumin, stir, and roast for 20 seconds. Add curry leaves and fried onions and mix well. Add rice and stir-fry for 1 minute.

Season with salt to taste and garnish with cilantro.

SERVES 4–6

3 Tbsp vegetable oil

1½ tsp black mustard seeds

12 curry leaves

3 dried red chiles, snapped in half

1 Tbsp split and hulled black gram (*urad dal*)

3–4 tomatoes, puréed (2 cups)

½ tsp salt

4 cups cooked basmati rice

Cilantro, coarsely chopped, for garnish

Fried Onions (page 42), for garnish

Tomato Rice

ടൊമാറ്റോ റൈസ്

If you have a summer crop of tomatoes, this is the perfect rice. Flavored and colored with tomatoes, red chiles, fried onions, and spices, tomato rice is a mainstay dish for vegetarian Hindus, and is often eaten with a bowl of yogurt and pickles. It's also a tasty way to spice up leftover rice.

HAVE A SPLASH guard and measured spices nearby. Heat oil in a small frying pan over medium-high heat until nearly smoking. Immediately reduce heat to medium. (You can test the heat of the oil by dropping in a couple of seeds. The oil is at the correct temperature when the seeds crackle, but do not burn.) Add mustard seeds and temper for a few seconds, until they stop popping. (Cover with the splash guard, if needed.) Add curry leaves, chiles, and black gram and cook for 15–30 seconds more, until the leaves curl. Transfer the spices to a large heavy-bottomed skillet.

Increase the heat to high. Pour in puréed tomatoes and salt and sauté for 3 minutes, until the liquid has evaporated. Reduce heat to medium. Add rice and mix well, until rice is completely coated.

Garnish with cilantro and fried onions.

> **Tempering** is a traditional method of extracting optimal flavor from Indian spices, and it is a skill learned with practice! Reducing the heat a little before adding the spices prevents the spices from burning and adding a bitterness to your dish. If they do burn, simply start again with fresh spices.

1 Tbsp Ghee (page 41)

1 tsp black mustard seeds

10 curry leaves

2 dried red chiles, snapped in half

1 tsp split and hulled black gram (*urad dal*)

½ tsp ground turmeric

3 cups cooked basmati rice

1 Tbsp fresh lemon juice

Pinch of salt

1½ tsp cilantro leaves, for garnish

1 Tbsp Fried Onions (page 42), for garnish

SERVES 4

Lemon Rice

ലെമൺ റൈസ്

Because of the acid in the lemons, the rice will keep longer—travelers would take lemon rice or Curd Rice (page 161) on a train or bus journey to eat with pickles. Turmeric sets the color of the rice, while fried onions give it an earthy crunch. You can eat this hot with a fish or lamb dish or chilled as a rice salad.

HAVE A SPLASH guard and measured spices nearby. Heat ghee in a small frying pan over medium-high heat until nearly smoking. Immediately reduce heat to medium. (You can test the heat of the ghee by dropping in a couple of seeds. It is at the correct temperature when the seeds crackle, but do not burn.) Add mustard seeds and temper for a few seconds, until they stop popping. (Cover with the splash guard, if needed.) Immediately add curry leaves, chiles, and black gram and sauté for 1 minute. Add turmeric and stir for 1 more minute, until incorporated. Transfer the spices to a large heavy-bottomed skillet.

Add rice and lemon juice and sauté over medium heat until heated through. Season with salt.

Garnish with cilantro and fried onions.

Tempering is a traditional method of extracting optimal flavor from Indian spices, and it is a skill learned with practice! Reducing the heat a little before adding the spices prevents the spices from burning and adding a bitterness to your dish. If they do burn, simply start again with fresh spices.

SERVES 4

2 cups patna rice, washed

2½ Tbsp salt

2 cups plain yogurt

2 Tbsp finely chopped ginger

3 Indian or Thai green chiles, finely chopped

Pinch of asafetida powder

2 Tbsp coconut oil

1 Tbsp black mustard seeds

1 cup split and hulled black gram (*urad dal*)

20 curry leaves

2 Tbsp chopped cilantro, for garnish

Shredded carrot, for garnish

To serve
Mango Pickle (page 50) or Lemon and Date Pickle (page 51)

Curd Rice

കേർഡ് റൈസ്

What the West calls "yogurt," we call "curd" in India. This Kerala comfort dish, of equal parts yogurt and rice, is flavored with ginger, chiles, curry leaves, and spices. Cool and fiery, it's a protein-packed vegetarian go-to dish for cooling down on a hot day, and is traditionally served in a clay pot called a *chatti*. Because it requires no heating up, and travels well, my mother would always pack up a bowl of curd rice for my father's long train journeys.

COMBINE RICE AND 8 cups water in a large saucepan and bring to a boil. Reduce heat and simmer, stirring occasionally, for 30 minutes, until rice has a porridge-like consistency. Set aside to cool for 30 minutes, then stir in salt.

Add yogurt, ginger, chiles, and asafetida and mix well. Set aside.

Have a splash guard and measured spices nearby. Heat oil in a small frying pan over medium-high heat until nearly smoking. Immediately reduce heat to medium. (You can test the heat of the oil by dropping in a couple of seeds. The oil is at the correct temperature when the seeds crackle, but do not burn.) Add mustard seeds and temper for a few seconds, until they stop popping. (Cover with the splash guard, if needed.) Add black gram and curry leaves and cook for 30 seconds until black gram has turned a golden brown and leaves have crisped.

Pour spice mixture into rice and mix well. Chill in the fridge, then garnish with cilantro and carrot. Serve with a pickle.

> **Tempering** is a traditional method of extracting optimal flavor from Indian spices, and it is a skill learned with practice! Reducing the heat a little before adding the spices prevents the spices from burning and adding a bitterness to your dish. If they do burn, simply start again with fresh spices.

4 Tbsp Ghee
(page 41, divided)

Handful of raisins

Handful of raw cashew nuts

6 green cardamom pods

6 cloves

1 (1-inch) cinnamon stick

1 star anise

2 cups kaima or basmati rice, washed

2 tsp salt (divided)

1–2 Indian bay leaves (optional)

2 onions, finely chopped

4 Indian or Thai green chiles, halved lengthwise

2 Tbsp Ginger-Garlic Paste (page 42)

1½ tsp Garam Masala (page 41)

2 tomatoes, finely chopped

1½ lbs lamb shanks or 1 lb stewing lamb

Juice of 1 lime

2 Tbsp coarsely chopped mint

2 Tbsp coarsely chopped cilantro

¼ cup Fried Onions (page 42)

2 tsp rosewater

SERVES 6–8

Lamb Biryani

ലാമ്ബ് ബിരിയാണി

Traditionally served in a deep, wide-mouthed cooking vessel called a *handi* (or biryani pot), this festive party dish is typically reserved for weddings and other celebratory occasions. Slow-braised, the biryani is infused with warm spices, mint, and cilantro, layered with onion, and crowned with roasted cashews and raisins. It was my honor to serve this dish at the prime minister's residence in 2015.

HEAT 2 TBSP GHEE in a large saucepan over medium-high heat. Add raisins and cashews and roast for 1–2 minutes, stirring occasionally, until the nuts turn golden brown. (Keep an eye on the pan to prevent the raisins and cashews from burning.) Using a slotted spoon, remove the cashews and raisins and set aside.

Add cardamom, cloves, cinnamon, and star anise and roast in the residual ghee for 1 minute. Add rice and fry for 2–3 minutes until rice is well coated. Add 4 cups water, 1 tsp salt, and bay leaves (if using), and bring to a boil. Reduce heat to low, cover, and simmer for 15 minutes, stirring 2–3 times to prevent rice and spices from sticking and until all the water is absorbed. Set aside.

Heat the remaining 2 Tbsp ghee in a large frying pan over high heat. Add onions and chiles and sauté for 2 minutes. Add ginger-garlic paste and garam masala and cook for 2–3 minutes. Reduce heat to medium, add tomatoes, and cook for 1 minute. Add lamb and remaining 1 tsp salt and sauté for 1–2 minutes, allowing the meat to brown on all sides. Add 1 cup water and cook, covered, for 30–40 minutes, or until lamb is tender. Remove from heat. Stir in lime juice, mint, and cilantro. Set aside.

Preheat oven to 350°F.

In a large casserole dish, arrange a layer of rice, a layer of the lamb mixture, and a sprinkle of fried onions. Repeat two more times, ending with a layer of rice. Sprinkle the rice with rosewater, seal with two layers of aluminum foil, and bake for 10 minutes. Garnish with raisins and cashews.

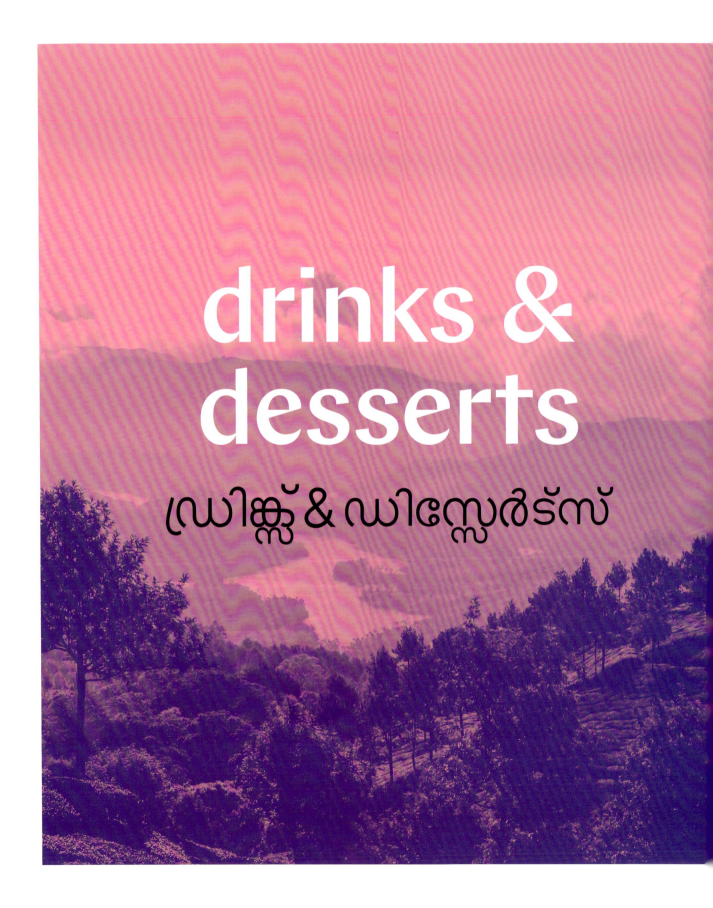

drinks & desserts

ഡ്രിങ്ക്സ് & ഡിസ്സേർട്സ്

166 **Mango Lassi**

167 **Lime–Poppy Seed Fizz**

168 **Sambaram**

171 **Cardamom Chai**

172 **Coconut and Jaggery Crepes**

174 **Rice Pudding**

175 **Semiya Payasam**

176 **Mango and Sago Mousse**

178 **Banana Fritters**

1 (1-inch) piece ginger, peeled

2 cups plain yogurt

¼ cup sugar

1½ cups fresh or canned mango pulp

SERVES 4

Mango Lassi
മാങ്ങ ലസ്സി

This marvelous mango milkshake is loved by young and old. Sweet and tangy, healthy and filling, it has a wonderfully potent mango flavor, and the ginger gives it an added zing! This recipe comes from my brother Majoe.

TO MAKE THE ginger juice, grate ginger into a small bowl. Using your fingers, squeeze the juice from the gratings. (Alternatively, grate the ginger into a piece of cheesecloth and squeeze the juice by twisting the cheesecloth tight.)

Combine 1½ Tbsp ginger juice and the remaining ingredients in a blender and purée until smooth. Pour over crushed ice.

SERVES 4

Simple syrup
½ cup sugar

Lime–poppy seed fizz
1 tsp poppy seeds
2 tsp fresh lime juice
¼ cup Simple Syrup (see here), plus extra to taste
6 cups club soda

Lime–Poppy Seed Fizz
നാരങ്ങ -പോപ്പി സീഡ് ഫീസ്

Poppy seeds grow in profusion in Kerala. Here, they're added to lime and soda, then the drink is sweetened with a little simple syrup and served over ice. Kids love this thirst-quencher: it's cool and refreshing, and the seeds pop in the mouth, which makes it kind of fun!

Simple syrup Combine ½ cup water and sugar together in a small saucepan and bring to a boil. Stir until sugar has dissolved, then set aside to cool.

Lime–poppy seed fizz In a small bowl, combine poppy seeds and ½ cup water and soak for 1 hour.

In a large pitcher, combine lime juice, simple syrup, and poppy seeds and their soaking water and mix well. Pour in club soda, mix, and serve chilled.

4 cups plain yogurt

1 tsp salt

2 Tbsp chopped ginger

3 Indian or Thai green chiles, finely chopped

12 curry leaves

SERVES 4

Sambaram

സംഭാരം

On scorching-hot Kerala days, you'll see sambaram sold everywhere at road-side stands. Salty and spicy, with a ginger pow, this lassi-like drink is made with fresh buttermilk, which really gives it a tang. We don't like the quality of commercial buttermilk here, so we use plain yogurt. For me, it's the perfect drink for cooling down after mowing the lawn in the sizzling summer sun.

COMBINE ALL INGREDIENTS in a blender and purée until smooth. Serve over ice.

SERVES 4

1½ Tbsp loose-leaf black tea

Sugar, to taste (optional)

4 green cardamom pods, crushed in a mortar and pestle

1 (½-inch) piece ginger, peeled and coarsely chopped

2 cups milk

Cardamom Chai

ഏലം ചായ

The comforting scent of my mother's chai wafting through our home, greeting my brothers and me after school, is one I treasure. Cardamom must dominate the flavor, so we use both seeds and pods, crushing them lightly and infusing the tea leaves with their gentle perfume. In India, we like our chai sweet, and we tend to boil the tea leaves with lots of sugar.

And by the way, chai means "tea." To order "chai tea" is redundant, like saying "I'll have a tea tea." If you learn only one thing from this book, learn that! Chai is chai.

BRING 2 CUPS WATER to boil in a small saucepan. Add tea leaves, sugar (if you like it sweet), crushed cardamom pods, and ginger and boil for 2 minutes to release the flavors. Pour in milk and bring back to a boil. Simmer for another 2 minutes.

Strain tea, then pour it from one jug to another, to create a froth, in turn creating a lighter tea. Serve hot.

MAKES 12–14

Jaggery syrup
2 cups jaggery or muscovado or dark brown sugar

Coconut filling
4 cups fresh or frozen grated coconut

1½ cups Jaggery Syrup (see here)

1½ tsp ground cardamom

⅓ cup cashews (optional)

⅓ cup raisins (optional)

Crepes
2½ cups all-purpose flour

2½ tsp sugar

¼ tsp salt

2½ cups milk

2 eggs

1 Tbsp coconut oil

To serve
Fresh mint leaves, for garnish (optional)

Fresh fruit or a fruit coulis (optional)

Coconut and Jaggery Crepes
തേങ്ങ ശർക്കര ക്രെപ്സ്

These crepes are proven to be addictive and they taste better when shared with friends. Rolled with spiced, sweet, and nutty coconut caramelized with jaggery syrup, this favorite after-school treat was often served with afternoon chai. If you can't source jaggery—a hardened block of sugar obtained from palm sap—use muscovado or dark brown sugar.

Jaggery syrup In a small saucepan, combine jaggery (or other sugar) and 1 cup water and bring to a boil. Reduce heat to medium and simmer for 8 minutes, stirring occasionally, until thickened. The syrup should be the consistency of honey. Set aside.

Coconut filling In a saucepan, combine grated coconut and jaggery syrup and caramelize over medium-low heat for 8 minutes, until the liquid has mostly evaporated and the mixture is almost dry. Stir in cardamom. Add cashews and raisins (if using) and set aside to cool.

Crepes In a large bowl, combine flour, sugar, and salt. Add milk, eggs, and oil. Using a hand blender or a whisk, mix until very smooth. Cover and set aside at room temperature for at least 20 minutes to rest.

Line a baking sheet with parchment paper. Heat a 6-inch-diameter nonstick frying pan over medium-high heat. Remove pan from the heat, then pour ¼ cup of batter into the pan, tilting and coating the pan evenly. Return to the heat and cook for 1 minute, until bubbles appear on the surface. Flip and cook for 1 more minute, until the edges turn golden brown. Transfer to the prepared baking sheet. Repeat with the remaining crepes until all the batter is used.

Spoon 2 Tbsp of the coconut mixture down the center of each crepe. Fold in both sides of the crepe, then roll it up to form a log. Eat them plain or serve topped with mint leaves and fresh fruit or fruit coulis.

1½ Tbsp Ghee (page 41)

Handful of raw cashew nuts

Handful of raisins

2 cups patna or basmati rice, thoroughly rinsed

2 cups coconut milk

½ cup condensed milk

1 cup sugar

6–8 green cardamom pods, crushed

SERVES 4–6

Rice Pudding

റൈസ് പുഡ്ഡിംഗ്

This classic Indian rice pudding is fragrant with cardamom and sweet coconut milk and festooned with roasted cashews and fried raisins. Typically served cold in Kerala, it's lovely warm on a wintry Canadian day.

HEAT GHEE IN a saucepan over medium-high heat. Add raisins and cashews and roast for 1–2 minutes, stirring occasionally, until the nuts turn golden brown. Using a slotted spoon, remove the cashews and raisins and set aside.

In a heavy-bottomed saucepan, combine rice, coconut milk, and 6 cups warm water and mix well. Bring to a boil, reduce heat to medium-low, and simmer for 20 minutes, until rice is well cooked.

Stir in condensed milk and sugar and bring back to a boil. Reduce heat and simmer for 2–3 minutes. Stir in cardamom.

Transfer pudding to a casserole dish or individual serving bowls. Sprinkle cashews and raisins overtop and serve immediately.

SERVES 4–6

1½ Tbsp ghee
Handful of raisins
Handful of raw cashew nuts
1 cup broken semiya (vermicelli pasta), in ½-inch lengths
4 cups milk
½ cup sugar
3 Tbsp condensed milk
1 tsp ground cardamom

Semiya Payasam

സേമിയ പായസം

This vermicelli milk pudding is a beloved Indian dessert. Made with toasted wheat vermicelli, milk, and sugar, it is laced with the delicate fragrance of cardamom and topped with ghee-roasted cashews and raisins. Served at feasts such as Onam sadya (page 80), semiya payasam is one of the easiest Indian desserts to make, and is always a comforting end to any meal. Served warm, it has the consistency of a runny custard. Chilled, it becomes a thick pudding.

HEAT GHEE IN a saucepan over medium-high heat. Add raisins and cashews and roast for 1–2 minutes, stirring occasionally, until the nuts turn golden brown. Using a slotted spoon, remove the cashews and raisins and set aside.

In the same saucepan, fry broken semiya over medium heat, until golden brown. Pour in 2 cups water, increase heat to medium-high, and cook for 3 minutes, stirring occasionally. Add milk, stir, and cook for another 4–5 minutes, until vermicelli is soft. Reduce heat to medium-low, add sugar, and stir for 1 more minute. Add condensed milk and simmer for 2 minutes, stirring occasionally.

Remove from heat. Stir in cardamom.

Garnish with raisins and cashews. Serve hot, warm, or chilled, depending on preference.

2 Tbsp gelatin powder

1 cup sago or tapioca pearls

4 cups milk

1 cup sugar

1½ cups fresh or canned mango pulp

To serve
Fresh fruit or a fruit coulis (optional)

SERVES 4

Mango and Sago Mousse
മംഗോ ആൻഡ് സാഗോ മൂസ്

Kerala kids take sago pudding to school or have it as a snack when they get home. Here, the pearls are cooked with milk, a bit of gelatin, and fresh mango pulp. You can make your own or buy it in a can from a gourmet food shop. Eat it straight up, or garnish with fresh fruit or a fruit coulis.

IN A SMALL bowl, combine gelatin and 3 Tbsp warm water and mix well to dissolve.

In a heavy-bottomed saucepan, combine sago (or tapioca) and 7 cups water and bring to a boil over medium-high heat. Cook for 20 minutes, until tender.

Pour milk into the pan and simmer for 2 minutes. Remove from heat and set aside to cool for 10 minutes. Add gelatin mixture and stir well. Stir in sugar. When cool, fold in mango pulp. Transfer pudding to a large serving bowl (or individual bowls) and chill in fridge, covered, for 3–6 hours, until firm.

Garnish with fresh fruit or a fruit coulis, if desired, and serve.

½ cup all-purpose flour

1½ Tbsp rice flour

2 Tbsp sugar

Pinch of salt

½ tsp cumin seeds

Pinch of turmeric

¾ tsp baking powder

2 ripe plantains or firm bananas

Canola oil, for frying

Cinnamon sugar, for dusting (optional)

SERVES 4

Banana Fritters

പഴം പൊരി

Sweet and slightly crisp, yet soft, you find these cumin-studded fritters sold in tea stalls throughout Kerala. We use ripe plantains for this dessert, but you could use firm bananas as well.

IN A LARGE bowl, combine flours, sugar, salt, cumin, turmeric, and baking powder. Add ¾ cup water and whisk until smooth. (It should have the consistency of pancake batter. Add more water if necessary.) Set aside.

Peel plantains (or bananas) and halve lengthwise. Cut each piece crosswise into three even slices (for 12 pieces total).

Heat oil in a deep-fryer or deep saucepan over medium-high heat, until it reaches a temperature of 370°F. Dip the sliced plantains, one by one, into the batter and carefully lower them into the hot oil (taking care not to splash). Fry in batches to avoid overcrowding, always making sure to bring the oil back to temperature before adding more slices. Using a slotted spoon, turn them gently and continuously until golden brown on all sides. Transfer fritters to a plate lined with paper towels and drain excess oil.

Dust with cinnamon sugar (if using) and serve immediately.

Metric Conversion Chart

VOLUME

Imperial or U.S.	Metric
⅛ tsp	0.5 ml
¼ tsp	1 ml
½ tsp	2.5 ml
¾ tsp	4 ml
1 tsp	5 ml
1 Tbsp	15 ml
1½ Tbsp	23 ml
2 Tbsp	30 ml
¼ cup	60 ml
⅓ cup	80 ml
½ cup	125 ml
⅔ cup	165 ml
¾ cup	185 ml
1 cup	250 ml
1¼ cups	310 ml
1⅓ cups	330 ml
1½ cups	375 ml
1⅔ cups	415 ml
1¾ cups	435 ml
2 cups	500 ml
2¼ cups	560 ml
2⅓ cups	580 ml
2½ cups	625 ml
2¾ cups	690 ml
3 cups	750 ml
4 cups	1 L
5 cups	1.25 L
6 cups	1.5 L
7 cups	1.75 L
8 cups	2 L

WEIGHT

Imperial or U.S.	Metric
½ oz	15 g
1 oz	30 g
2 oz	60 g
3 oz	85 g
4 oz (¼ lb)	115 g
5 oz	140 g
6 oz	170 g
7 oz	200 g
8 oz (½ lb)	225 g
9 oz	255 g
10 oz	285 g
11 oz	310 g
12 oz (¾ lb)	340 g
13 oz	370 g
14 oz	400 g
15 oz	425 g
16 oz (1 lb)	450 g
1¼ lbs	570 g
1½ lbs	670 g
2 lbs	900 g
3 lbs	1.4 kg
4 lbs	1.8 kg
5 lbs	2.3 kg
6 lbs	2.7 kg

CANS AND JARS

Imperial or U.S.	Metric
14 oz	398 ml
28 oz	796 ml

LINEAR

Imperial or U.S.	Metric
⅛ inch	3 mm
¼ inch	6 mm
½ inch	12 mm
¾ inch	2 cm
1 inch	2.5 cm
1¼ inches	3 cm
1½ inches	3.5 cm
1¾ inches	4.5 cm
2 inches	5 cm
2½ inches	6.5 cm
3 inches	7.5 cm
4 inches	10 cm
5 inches	12.5 cm
6 inches	15 cm
7 inches	18 cm
8 inches	20 cm
9 inches	23 cm
10 inches	25 cm
11 inches	28 cm
12 inches (1 foot)	30 cm
13 inches	33 cm
18 inches	46 cm

TEMPERATURE
(for oven temperatures, see list at right)

Imperial or U.S.	Metric
90°F	32°C
120°F	49°C
125°F	52°C
130°F	54°C
135°F	57°C
140°F	60°C
145°F	63°C
150°F	66°C
155°F	68°C
160°F	71°C
165°F	74°C
170°F	77°C
175°F	80°C
180°F	82°C
185°F	85°C
190°F	88°C
195°F	91°C
200°F	93°C
225°F	107°C
250°F	121°C
275°F	135°C
300°F	149°C
325°F	163°C
350°F	177°C
360°F	182°C
375°F	191°C

OVEN TEMPERATURE

Imperial or U.S.	Metric
200°F	95°C
250°F	120°C
275°F	135°C
300°F	150°C
325°F	160°C
350°F	180°C
375°F	190°C
400°F	200°C
425°F	220°C
450°F	230°C

Acknowledgments

MY FIRST BIG *nandi* must go to the loving and loyal guests who walk through our doors every day, and without whom there would be no Coconut Lagoon. I'd also like to extend my gratitude to my restaurant team, just as loving and loyal—many have been with me since the very beginning. Special recognition to my dear brothers Majoe and Thomas Thottungal, and to Sudeep Jose and to their families; to Malkit Singh, my front-of-house all-star; and to my long-serving chef de cuisine, Rajesh Gopi. Thanks as well to Makori, Myint ta, Renju, Willio, Yassein, Saji, Yoga, Tenzin, Dawa, and Neh Kare.

Thank you to my true and steady companions on this cookbook adventure: to my co-author, Anne DesBrisay, who helped put my life and thoughts and ideas into words. To our editor, Michelle Meade, and copy editor, Pam Robertson, for their sharp eyes, endless patience, and enthusiasm for this project. And thanks to Figure 1's brilliant designer, Naomi MacDougall, for marrying the images and words in these handsome pages.

I have received over many years, and am most grateful for, the professional help and support from the Ottawa culinary and restaurant community. I'd also like to extend my gratitude to Stephen Beckta, Gay Cook, Patrick Garland, Vikas Khanna, Marc Lepine, Mary Wetscher, Wilhelm Wetscher, and Sheila Whyte. Thank you. Chefs I admire and respect from other parts of the world did us the honor of flying in to cook with us—thank you Vikram Vij, Peter Joseph, and Milton Rebello.

I met photographer Christian Lalonde during the creation of *Ottawa Cooks* and was astonished at his unique and energetic images. How wonderful that he was free to lend his considerable talents to this book, and that he came with food stylist Sylvie Benoit and prop stylist Irene Garavelli. The beautiful images of Kerala are a gift from my friend Jonathan Barker.

To my network of amateur but avid cooks, who tested with enthusiasm and generosity a random selection of recipes—your constructive criticisms led to important tweaks to these pages. Thank you.

Nandi Amma and Appa, my mum and dad in Kerala, who have supported my aspirations and my Canadian cooking career, always, and to my wonderful Ottawa family—my loving wife, Suma, and our beautiful children, Marieann, Mathew, and Michael Thottungal.

And finally, I honor my grandfather, TJ Francis, and his words of advice and encouragement: "Remember, Joe, if you are filling someone's stomach well, you are also filling their hearts."

Resources

My hope is for you to recreate authentic dishes with ease, but I understand that some ingredients may not be readily available in some regions. If you're looking for fresh ingredients and/or pantry essentials, I recommend the following online resources.

AUSTRALIA

Hindustan Imports
www.hindustan.com.au

India at Home
www.indiaathome.com.au

India Bazaar
www.indiabazaar.com.au

CANADA

Apniroots
www.apniroots.com

Singal's
www.singals.ca

The Spice Trader
www.thespicetrader.ca

Spice Trekkers
www.spicetrekkers.com

UNITED STATES

Grocery Babu
www.grocerybabu.com

iShop Indian
www.ishopindian.com

Khana Pakana
shop.khanapakana.com

UNITED KINGDOM

The Asian Cookshop
www.theasiancookshop.co.uk

Red Rickshaw
www.redrickshaw.com

Spices of India
www.spicesofindia.co.uk

Index

Page numbers in *italics* refer to photos. Page numbers in **bold** refer to ingredient descriptions or definitions.

ADZUKI BEANS (RED COWPEAS), **22**, *25*
  in pumpkin erissery, 94
AJWAIN. *See* carom seeds (ajwain)
appam, 54
ASAFETIDA POWDER, **22**, *28–29*
  in carrot pickle, 47
  in curd rice, 161
  in lemon and date pickle, 51
  in mango pickle, 50
  in parippu vadas, 69
ATTA, **22**
  in chapatis, 55
  in pooris, 59
aviyal, mushroom, *81*, 100

baby eggplant masala, *81*, *104*, 105
BANANA LEAVES, **22**
  fish roasted in, 118, *119*
BANANA(S)
  fritters, 178
  in mezhukkupuratti, 90
BASMATI RICE, **36**, 156
  in appam, 54
  in jeera rice, 158
  in lamb biryani, 162
  in lemon rice, 160
  in rice pudding, 174
  in tomato rice, 159
BEANS. *See* adzuki beans (red cowpeas); green beans. *See also* dal (dahl); peas

BEEF
  curry, 146, *147*
  fry, Kerala, 144, *145*
BELL PEPPER. *See* green bell pepper; red bell pepper, in crab cakes
BENGAL GRAM. *See* chana dal (Bengal gram)
black chickpea salad, 84, *85*
BLACK GRAM (URAD), **22**, *25*
  in cabbage thoran, 87
  in carrot and coconut foogath, 93
  in coconut chutney, 44
  in curd rice, 161
  in dosas, 56
  in lemon rice, 160
  in potato masala, 101
  in scallops with tomato chutney, 74
  in tomato rice, 159
BLACK MUSTARD SEEDS, **22–23**, *28–29*
  in coconut chutney, 44
  in curd rice, 161
  in mango pickle, 50
BLACK PEPPER, **23**
  in chicken Chettinad, 134
  in Kerala beef fry, 144
  in Malabar pepper lamb, 151
BREAD
  appam, 54
  chapatis, 55
  dosas, 56, *57*
  Malabar parathas, 60, *61*
  pooris, *58*, 59
BREADCRUMBS. *See* panko breadcrumbs
broccoli thoran, *88*, 89

butter chicken, Coconut Lagoon, *138*, 139
BUTTERNUT SQUASH, in pumpkin erissery, 94

CABBAGE
  in Kerala-style slaw, 83
  thoran, *81*, 87
  in vegetable kuchumber, 86
CARDAMOM. *See* green cardamom
CAROM SEEDS (AJWAIN), **23**, *28–29*
  in pooris, 59
CARROT
  in black chickpea salad, 84
  in cabbage thoran, 87
  and coconut foogath, 93
  in Kerala-style slaw, 83
  in Kerala-style vegetable stew, 97
  in nadan vegetable korma, 98
  pickle, 47, *48–49*
  in potato masala, 101
  in sweet potato and ginger soup, 65
  in vegetable kuchumber, 86
CASHEW NUTS, **23**
  in chicken Chettinad, 134
  in coconut and jaggery crepes, 172
  in Coconut Lagoon butter chicken, 139
  in Kerala-style vegetable stew, 97
  in lamb biryani, 162
  in rice pudding, 174
  in semiya payasam, 175

CAULIFLOWER
    in Kerala-style vegetable
        stew, 97
    masala, 102, *103*
    in nadan vegetable
        korma, 98
CHAAT MASALA, **23**, *28–29*
    in Coconut Lagoon butter
        chicken, 139
    in vegetable kuchumber, 86
chai, cardamom, *170*, 171
CHANA DAL (BENGAL GRAM), **23**, *25*
    in dosas, 56
    in parippu vadas, 69
chapatis, 55
Chettinad masala, 134
CHICKEN
    butter, Coconut Lagoon, *138*, 139
    Chettinad, 134
    in cook's curry, 135
    in nadan kozhi curry, 136
    Nilgiri, 140, *141*
CHICKPEA(S), **23**, *25*. *See also* chana dal (Bengal gram)
    curry, 109
    salad, black, 84, *85*
CHILES. *See* green chiles; red chiles
chili-lime sauce, 43, *48–49*
CHILI POWDER. *See* Kashmiri chili powder; red chili powder
CHUTNEY
    coconut, 44, *48–49*
    mint, 45, *48–49*
    tomato, scallops with, 74
CILANTRO
    in curd rice, 161
    in lamb biryani, 162
    in Malabar pepper lamb, 151
    in mint chutney, 45
    in Nilgiri chicken, 140
    in vegetable kuchumber, 86
CINNAMON, **24**, *28–29*
    in chicken Chettinad, 134
    in duck Kumarakom, 143
    in garam masala, 41
    in Kerala-style vegetable stew, 97
    in lamb biryani, 162
    in nadan kozhi curry, 136
    in Nilgiri chicken, 140
    in Ooty mushroom curry, 113
CLAMATO JUICE, in Coconut Lagoon mussels, 125
CLOVES, **24**, *28–29*
    in chicken Chettinad, 134
    in garam masala, 41
    in Kerala-style vegetable stew, 97
    in lamb biryani, 162
    in nadan kozhi curry, 136
    in Nilgiri chicken, 140
    in Ooty mushroom curry, 113
CLUB SODA, in lime–poppy seed fizz, 167
COCONUT, *32*, **33**–34, *35*. *See also* coconut cream; coconut milk; coconut vinegar
    in appam, 54
    in broccoli thoran, 89
    in cabbage thoran, 87
    and carrot foogath, 93
    chutney, 44, *48–49*
    and jaggery crepes, 172, *173*
    in Kerala beef fry, 144
    in mushroom aviyal, 100
    paste, 152
    in pineapple pachadi, 46
    in pumpkin erissery, 94
    in shrimp Malabar, 126
    in squid peera, 75
COCONUT CREAM, **33**
    in Coconut Lagoon mussels, 125
    in Nilgiri chicken, 140
Coconut Lagoon butter chicken, *138*, 139
Coconut Lagoon mussels, *124*, 125
COCONUT MILK, **33**
    in beef curry, 146
    in chickpea curry, 109
    in duck Kumarakom, 143
    in egg mappas, 108
    in fish roasted in banana leaf, 118
    in Kerala-style vegetable stew, 97
    in lamb korma, 152
    in lobster masala, 131
    in mango curry, 110
    in masoor dal and spinach curry, 114
    in nadan kozhi curry, 136
    in nadan vegetable korma, 98
    in Ooty mushroom curry, 113
    in rice pudding, 174
    in shrimp mango curry, 130
    in sweet potato and ginger soup, 65
    in Thrissur-style salmon curry, 122
    in Travancore fish curry, 121
COCONUT VINEGAR, **34**
    in Kerala-style slaw, 83
    in mango curry, 110
COD, in Travancore fish curry, 121
CONDIMENTS
    carrot pickle, 47, *48–49*
    chili-lime sauce, 43, *48–49*

coconut chutney, 44, 48–49
ginger-garlic paste, 42
Kerala raita, 43, 48–49
lemon and date pickle,
    48–49, 51, *81*
mango pickle, 48–49, 50, *81*
mint chutney, 45, 48–49
pineapple pachadi, 46,
    48–49, *81*
tamarind paste, 64, 76,
    100, 105, 129
cook's curry, 135
CORIANDER, **24**, *28–29*
    in baby eggplant masala, 105
    in beef curry, 146
    in cauliflower masala, 102
    in chicken Chettinad, 134
    in cook's curry, 135
    in duck Kumarakom, 143
    in Kerala beef fry, 144
    in lamb korma, 152
    in lamb with fennel seeds, 149
    in Malabar pepper lamb, 151
    in nadan kozhi curry, 136
    in Nilgiri chicken, 140
    in Ooty mushroom curry, 113
crab cakes, 70, *71*
crepes, coconut and
    jaggery, 172, *173*
croquettes, potato and
    spinach, 66, *67*
CUCUMBER, in vegetable
    kuchumber, 86
CUMIN, **24**–**26**, *28–29*
    in carrot and coconut
        foogath, 93
    in chicken Chettinad, 134
    in jeera rice, 158
    in masoor dal and
        spinach curry, 114
    in mushroom aviyal, 100

CURD. *See* yogurt (curd)
CURRY. *See also* korma; stew
    beef, 146, *147*
    chicken Chettinad, 134
    chickpea, 109
    Coconut Lagoon butter
        chicken, *138*, 139
    duck Kumarakom, 143
    mango, 110, *111*
    masoor dal and spinach,
        114, *115*
    Nilgiri chicken, 140
    Ooty mushroom, *112*, 113
    shrimp mango, 130
    Thrissur-style salmon,
        122, *123*
    Travancore fish, *120*, 121
CURRY LEAVES, **36**
    in baby eggplant masala, 105
    in beef curry, 146
    in broccoli thoran, 89
    in cabbage thoran, 87
    in carrot and coconut
        foogath, 93
    in carrot pickle, 47
    in cauliflower masala, 102
    in chicken Chettinad, 134
    in chickpea curry, 109
    in coconut chutney, 44
    in Coconut Lagoon
        mussels, 125
    in cook's curry, 135
    in crab cakes, 70
    in curd rice, 161
    in dal masala, 107
    in egg mappas, 108
    in fish roasted in
        banana leaf, 118
    in jeera rice, 158
    in Kerala beef fry, 144
    in Kerala lamb chops, 76

    in Kerala raita, 43
    in Kerala-style vegetable
        stew, 97
    in lamb with fennel
        seeds, 149
    in lemon rice, 160
    in lobster masala, 131
    in Malabar pepper lamb, 151
    in mango curry, 110
    in masoor dal and
        spinach curry, 114
    in mushroom aviyal, 100
    in nadan kozhi curry, 136
    in Ooty mushroom curry, 113
    in parippu vadas, 69
    in pineapple pachadi, 46
    in potato masala, 101
    in pumpkin erissery, 94
    in rasam, 64
    in sambaram, 168
    in scallops with tomato
        chutney, 74
    in shrimp kakkan, 73
    in shrimp Malabar, 126
    in shrimp mango
        curry, 130
    in squid peera, 75
    in tamarind shrimp
        masala, 129
    in Thrissur-style salmon
        curry, 122
    in tomato rice, 159
    in Travancore fish curry, 121
    in vegetable kuchumber, 86

DAL (DAHL), *25*, **26**. *See also*
    beans; black gram (urad);
    chana dal (Bengal gram);
    chickpea(s); peas; red
    lentils (masoor dal)
    masala, 107

Index 187

date and lemon pickle,
    48–49, 51, 81
DESSERTS
    banana fritters, 178
    coconut and jaggery crepes,
        172, 173
    mango and sago mousse,
        176, 177
    rice pudding, 174
    semiya payasam, 175
dosas, 56, 57
DRINKS
    cardamom chai, 170, 171
    lime–poppy seed fizz, 167
    mango lassi, 166
    sambaram, 81, 168, 169
duck Kumarakom, 143

egg mappas, 108
eggplant masala, 81, 104, 105
erissery, pumpkin, 81, 94, 95

FENNEL SEEDS, 26, 28–29
    in chicken Chettinad, 134
    in duck Kumarakom, 143
    in egg mappas, 108
    in garam masala, 41
    lamb with, 148, 149
    in scallops with tomato
        chutney, 74
FENUGREEK LEAVES (KASURI
        METHI), 26, 28–29
    in Coconut Lagoon
        butter chicken, 139
    in Ooty mushroom curry, 113
    in potato and spinach
        croquettes, 66
FENUGREEK SEEDS
    in carrot pickle, 47
    in dosas, 56
    in mango pickle, 50

FISH
    curry, Travancore, 120, 121
    roasted in banana leaf, 118, 119
    salmon curry, Thrissur-style,
        122, 123
foogath, carrot and coconut, 93
FRIED ONIONS, 42
    in jeera rice, 158
    in lamb biryani, 162
    in lemon rice, 160
    in tomato rice, 159
fritters, banana, 178

GARAM MASALA, 26,
        28–29, 48–49
    in beef curry, 146
    in cauliflower masala, 102
    in coconut paste, 152
    in cook's curry, 135
    in crab cakes, 70
    in Kerala beef fry, 144
    in Kerala lamb chops, 76
    in lamb biryani, 162
    in lamb korma, 152
    in nadan kozhi curry, 136
GARLIC, 26. See also ginger-
        garlic paste
    in chili-lime sauce, 43
    in Coconut Lagoon
        mussels, 125
    in cook's curry, 135
    -ginger paste. See ginger-
        garlic paste
    in mango pickle, 50
    in mint chutney, 45
    in nadan kozhi curry, 136
    in Ooty mushroom
        curry, 113
    in Thrissur-style salmon
        curry, 122
    in Travancore fish curry, 121

GELATIN, in mango and sago
    mousse, 176
GHEE, 26, 41, 81
GINGER, 26. See also ginger-
        garlic paste
    in cardamom chai, 171
    in chickpea curry, 109
    in coconut chutney, 44
    in Coconut Lagoon
        mussels, 125
    in cook's curry, 135
    in curd rice, 161
    in duck Kumarakom, 143
    -garlic paste. See ginger-
        garlic paste
    in Kerala beef fry, 144
    in Kerala-style vegetable
        stew, 97
    in lamb korma, 152
    in lamb with fennel seeds, 149
    in mango curry, 110
    in mango lassi, 166
    in mango pickle, 50
    in masoor dal and
        spinach curry, 114
    in nadan kozhi curry, 136
    in Ooty mushroom curry, 113
    in parippu vadas, 69
    in pineapple pachadi, 46
    in potato masala, 101
    in pumpkin erissery, 94
    in sambaram, 168
    in shrimp kakkan, 73
    in shrimp mango curry, 130
    in squid peera, 75
    and sweet potato soup, 65
    in tamarind shrimp
        masala, 129
    in Thrissur-style salmon
        curry, 122
    in Travancore fish curry, 121

GINGER-GARLIC PASTE, 42
    in baby eggplant masala, 105
    in beef curry, 146
    in cauliflower masala, 102
    in chicken Chettinad, 134
    in egg mappas, 108
    in fish roasted in banana leaf, 118
    in Kerala lamb chops, 76
    in lamb biryani, 162
    in lemon and date pickle, 51
    in Malabar pepper lamb, 151
    in Nilgiri chicken, 140
GRAM. *See* black gram (urad); chana dal (Bengal gram); chickpea(s)
GRAPES, in pineapple pachadi, 46
GREEN BEANS
    in Kerala-style vegetable stew, 97
    in nadan vegetable korma, 98
GREEN BELL PEPPER
    in black chickpea salad, 84
    in crab cakes, 70
    in Kerala-style slaw, *82*, 83
    in lamb with fennel seeds, 149
    in vegetable kuchumber, 86
GREEN CARDAMOM, **23**, *28–29*
    chai, *170*, 171
    in coconut and jaggery crepes, 172
    in duck Kumarakom, 143
    in garam masala, 41
    in Kerala-style vegetable stew, 97
    in lamb biryani, 162
    in nadan kozhi curry, 136
    in Nilgiri chicken, 140
    in Ooty mushroom curry, 113
    in rice pudding, 174
    in semiya payasam, 175

GREEN CHILES, **23**
    in beef curry, 146
    in broccoli thoran, 89
    in carrot pickle, 47
    in cauliflower masala, 102
    in chickpea curry, 109
    in coconut chutney, 44
    in Coconut Lagoon mussels, 125
    in cook's curry, 135
    in curd rice, 161
    in duck Kumarakom, 143
    in egg mappas, 108
    in fish roasted in banana leaf, 118
    in Kerala raita, 43
    in Kerala-style slaw, 83
    in Kerala-style vegetable stew, 97
    in lamb biryani, 162
    in lamb korma, 152
    in lobster masala, 131
    in mango curry, 110
    in masoor dal and spinach curry, 114
    in mezhukkupuratti, 90
    in mint chutney, 45
    in mushroom aviyal, 100
    in nadan kozhi curry, 136
    in nadan vegetable korma, 98
    in Nilgiri chicken, 140
    in parippu vadas, 69
    in potato masala, 101
    in pumpkin erissery, 94
    in sambaram, 168
    in squid peera, 75
    in Thrissur-style salmon curry, 122
    in Travancore fish curry, 121
    in vegetable kuchumber, 86

INDIAN BAY LEAVES (TEJ PATTA), **27**, *28–29*
    in lamb biryani, 162

JAGGERY, **27**
    and coconut crepes, 172, *173*
    syrup, 173
    jeera rice, 158

KAIMA RICE, in lamb biryani, 162
kala chana (black chickpea) salad, 84
KASHMIRI CHILI POWDER, **27**, *28–29*
    in carrot pickle, 47
    in lobster masala, 131
    in shrimp kakkan, 73
    in Travancore fish curry, 121
KASURI METHI. *See* fenugreek leaves (kasuri methi)
Kerala beef fry, 144, *145*
Kerala lamb chops, 76, *77*
Kerala raita, 43, *48–49*
Kerala-style slaw, *82*, 83
Kerala-style vegetable stew, *81*, *96*, 97
KORMA
    lamb, 152, *153*
    nadan vegetable, 98, *99*
kuchumber, vegetable, 86
KUDAMPULI (MALABAR TAMARIND), **27**
    in Coconut Lagoon mussels, 125
    in lobster masala, 131
    in shrimp Malabar, 126
    in squid peera, 75
    in Thrissur-style salmon curry, 122
    in Travancore fish curry, 121

LAMB
    biryani, 162, *163*
    chops, Kerala, 76, *77*
    with fennel seeds, *148*, 149
    korma, 152, *153*
    Malabar pepper, 151
lassi, mango, 166
LEMON
    and date pickle, *48–49*, 51, *81*
    rice, 160
LENTILS. *See* black gram (urad); chana dal (Bengal gram); chickpea(s); red lentils (masoor dal)
LIME
    -chili sauce, 43, *48–49*
    in lamb biryani, 162
    –poppy seed fizz, 167
lobster masala, 131

Malabar parathas, 60, *61*
Malabar pepper lamb, 151
Malabar shrimp, 126
MALABAR TAMARIND. *See* kudampuli (Malabar tamarind)
MANGO, **27**
    curry, 110, *111*
    lassi, 166
    pickle, *48–49*, 50, *81*
    and sago mousse, 176, *177*
    shrimp curry, 130
mappas, egg, 108
MASALA. *See also* chaat masala; Chettinad masala; garam masala
    baby eggplant, *81*, *104*, 105
    cauliflower, 102, *103*
    chana (chickpea curry), 109
    dal, *81*, 107
    lobster, 131

    potato, 101
    tamarind shrimp, *128*, 129
MASOOR DAL. *See* red lentils (masoor dal)
Matta rice, **36**, *81*, 157
MAYONNAISE
    in chili-lime sauce, 43
    in crab cakes, 70
mezhukkupuratti, 90, *91*
MINT
    chutney, 45, *48–49*
    in lamb biryani, 162
    in Nilgiri chicken, 140
mousse, mango and sago, 176, *177*
MUSHROOM
    aviyal, *81*, 100
    curry, *112*, 113
MUSSELS, Coconut Lagoon, *124*, 125
MUSTARD SEEDS. *See* black mustard seeds

nadan kozhi curry, 136, *137*
nadan vegetable korma, 98, *99*
Nilgiri chicken, 140, *141*
NUTS. *See* cashew nuts

ONIONS, **27**
    in baby eggplant masala, 105
    in beef curry, 146
    in broccoli thoran, 89
    in cabbage thoran, 87
    in carrot and coconut foogath, 93
    in cauliflower masala, 102
    in chicken Chettinad, 134
    in coconut chutney, 44
    in Coconut Lagoon butter chicken, 139

    in Coconut Lagoon mussels, 125
    in cook's curry, 135
    in dal masala, 107
    in duck Kumarakom, 143
    in egg mappas, 108
    fried. *See* fried onions
    in Kerala beef fry, 144
    in lamb biryani, 162
    in lamb korma, 152
    in lamb with fennel seeds, 149
    in lobster masala, 131
    in Malabar pepper lamb, 151
    in masoor dal and spinach curry, 114
    in mint chutney, 45
    in nadan kozhi curry, 136
    in Nilgiri chicken, 140
    in Ooty mushroom curry, 113
    in potato masala, 101
    red, in black chickpea salad, 84
    red, in Kerala raita, 43
    red, in vegetable kuchumber, 86
    in tamarind shrimp masala, 129
Ooty mushroom curry, *112*, 113

pachadi, pineapple, 46, *48–49*, *81*
PANKO BREADCRUMBS
    for crab cakes, 70
    for potato and spinach croquettes, 66
parathas, Malabar, 60, *61*
parippu vadas, *68*, 69
PASTE
    coconut, 152
    ginger-garlic. *See* ginger-garlic paste
    tamarind, 64, 76, 100, 105, 129

PATNA RICE, **36**
    in appam, 54
    in curd rice, 161
    in dosas, 56
    in rice pudding, 174
PEAS
    in Kerala-style vegetable
        stew, 97
    in nadan vegetable korma, 98
peera, squid, 75
pepper lamb, Malabar, 151
PICKLE
    carrot, 47, 48–49
    lemon and date, 48–49, 51, *81*
    mango, 48–49, 50, *81*
pineapple pachadi, 46, 48–49, *81*
PLANTAIN
    fritters, 178
    in mezhukkupuratti, 90
pooris, *58*, 59
POPPY SEED(S), **27**
    –lime fizz, 167
POTATO(ES)
    in cauliflower masala, 102
    in Kerala-style vegetable
        stew, 97
    masala, 101
    in nadan vegetable korma, 98
    and spinach croquettes, *66*, 67
PUMPKIN, **30**
    erissery, *81*, *94*, 95

RAISINS
    in coconut and jaggery
        crepes, 172
    in Kerala-style vegetable
        stew, 97
    in lamb biryani, 162
    in rice pudding, 174
    in semiya payasam, 175
raita, Kerala, 43, *48–49*

rasam, 64
RED BELL PEPPER,
    in crab cakes, 70
RED CHILES, **24**
    in broccoli thoran, 89
    in cabbage thoran, 87
    in carrot and coconut
        foogath, 93
    in chicken Chettinad, 134
    in coconut chutney, 44
    in dal masala, 107
    in Kerala beef fry, 144
    in lamb with fennel seeds, 149
    in lemon rice, 160
    in mango curry, 110
    in pineapple pachadi, 46
    in potato masala, 101
    in rasam, 64
    in scallops with tomato
        chutney, 74
    in tomato rice, 159
RED CHILI POWDER, *28–29*, **30**
    in beef curry, 146
    in Kerala beef fry, 144
    in lemon and date pickle, 51
    in Malabar pepper lamb, 151
    in mango pickle, 50
    in nadan kozhi curry, 136
RED COWPEAS. *See* adzuki beans
    (red cowpeas)
RED LENTILS (MASOOR DAL),
    25, **30**
    in dal masala, 107
    and spinach curry, 114
RED ONIONS. *See under* onions
RICE, **36**
    in appam, 54
    basmati. *See* basmati rice
    curd, 161
    in dosas, 56
    flour, in banana fritters, 178

    jeera, 158
    in lamb biryani, 162
    lemon, 160
    Matta, *81*, 157
    pudding, 174
    tomato, 159
ROSEWATER, **30**
    in lamb biryani, 162

sago and mango
    mousse, 176, *177*
SALAD
    black chickpea, 84, *85*
    Kerala-style slaw, *82*, 83
    vegetable kuchumber, 86
salmon curry, 122, *123*
sambaram, *81*, 168, *169*
sauce, chili-lime, 43, *48–49*
scallops with tomato
    chutney, 74
SEMIYA (VERMICELLI), **30**
    payasam, *81*, 175
SESAME OIL, **30**
    in lemon and date pickle, 51
    in mango pickle, 50
SHALLOTS
    in crab cakes, 70
    in fish roasted in
        banana leaf, 118
    in mango curry, 110
    in mezhukkupuratti, 90
    in mushroom aviyal, 100
    in shrimp Malabar, 126
    in squid peera, 75
SHRIMP
    kakkan, *72*, 73
    Malabar, 126, *127*
    mango curry, 130
    masala, tamarind, *128*, 129
simple syrup, 167
slaw, Kerala-style, *82*, 83

SOUP
  rasam, 64
  sweet potato and ginger, 65
SPINACH
  and masoor dal curry, 114, *115*
  and potato croquettes, 66, *67*
squid peera, 75
STAR ANISE, *28–29*, **30**
  in garam masala, 41
  in Kerala-style vegetable stew, 97
  in lamb biryani, 162
  in nadan kozhi curry, 136
  in Nilgiri chicken, 140
  in Ooty mushroom curry, 113
STEW. See also curry; korma
  Kerala-style vegetable, 96, *97*
  lamb biryani, 162, *163*
  Malabar pepper lamb, 151
  mushroom aviyal, 100
STIR-FRY. See also masala
  broccoli thoran, *88*, 89
  cabbage thoran, *81*, 87
  carrot and coconut foogath, 93
  Kerala beef fry, 144
  lamb with fennel seeds, 149
  mezhukkupuratti, 90, *91*
sweet potato and ginger soup, 65

TAMARIND, *28–29*, **30**. See also kudampuli (Malabar tamarind)
  in baby eggplant masala, 105
  in Kerala lamb chops, 76
  in mushroom aviyal, 100
  in rasam, 64
  shrimp masala, *128*, 129

TAPIOCA, **30**
  pearls, in mango and sago mousse, 176
tea, cardamom, *170*, 171
TEJ PATTA. See Indian bay leaves (tej patta)
THORAN
  broccoli, *88*, 89
  cabbage, *81*, 87
Thrissur-style salmon curry, 122, *123*
tilapia roasted in banana leaf, 118, *119*
TINDORA, **31**
  in mezhukkupuratti, 90
TOMATO(ES), **31**
  in baby eggplant masala, 105
  in beef curry, 146
  in cauliflower masala, 102
  in chicken Chettinad, 134
  in chickpea curry, 109
  chutney, scallops with, 74
  in Coconut Lagoon butter chicken, 139
  in cook's curry, 135
  in dal masala, 107
  in duck Kumarakom, 143
  in fish roasted in banana leaf, 118
  in Kerala raita, 43
  in lamb biryani, 162
  in lobster masala, 131
  in Malabar pepper lamb, 151
  in nadan kozhi curry, 136
  in Ooty mushroom curry, 113
  in rasam, 64
  rice, 159
  in tamarind shrimp masala, 129
  in Thrissur-style salmon curry, 122

  in vegetable kuchumber, 86
Travancore fish curry, 120, *121*
TURMERIC, *28–29*, **31**
  in beef curry, 146
  in chicken Chettinad, 134
  in cook's curry, 135
  in lemon rice, 160
  in Malabar pepper lamb, 151
  in mango pickle, 50
  in nadan vegetable korma, 98
  in Ooty mushroom curry, 113
  in shrimp kakkan, 73

URAD. See black gram (urad)

vadas, parippu, *68*, 69
VEGETABLE. See also individual vegetables
  korma, nadan, 98, *99*
  kuchumber, 86
  stew, Kerala-style, *81*, 96, *97*
VERMICELLI. See semiya (vermicelli)

YELLOW SPLIT PEAS. See chana dal (Bengal gram)
YOGURT (CURD), **31**
  in Coconut Lagoon butter chicken, 139
  in Kerala lamb chops, 76
  in Kerala raita, 43
  in mango lassi, 166
  in mint chutney, 45
  in Nilgiri chicken, 140
  in pineapple pachadi, 46
  rice, 161
  in sambaram, 168
  in shrimp kakkan, 73

ZUCCHINI, in mezhukkupuratti, 90